THE HEART HEALTHY COOKBOOK FOR BEGINNERS

Discover Lifelong Vitality - 2000 Days of Beginner-Friendly Low-Sodium, Low-Fat Recipes to Jumpstart Your Heart-Healthy Journey! Complete with a Step-by-Step 30-Day Meal Plan

Jillian Presley

Table of Contents

Introduction

Discover the pillars of a heart-healthy lifestyle

In a world that never sleeps, amidst the hustle of urban life, there lies an organ in our chest that tirelessly pumps life into our every moment. Our heart. As the central hub of our body's machinery, it deserves an unmatched level of attention and care. For many of us, particularly for those who've climbed the corporate ladder, focusing on heart health can be seen as a daunting task, surrounded by misinformation and myths. However, as we'll uncover, the foundation of a heart-healthy lifestyle is built upon simple yet effective pillars.

The first pillar of a heart-healthy lifestyle is knowledge. It sounds cliché, doesn't it? But consider this: How often do we buy gadgets or software without at least a cursory understanding of its specifications or how it operates? Similarly, we need to understand the workings of our heart. It's not just about knowing that it beats. It's about understanding how our daily choices—what we eat, how we move, the stress we endure—impact its functions. For the manager leading teams at a tech firm or the software engineer cracking the next big code, this knowledge is as crucial as understanding the latest technology trends.

Next, we come to nutrition. Forget the fad diets and the "magic" heart-healthy foods that pop up on our screens. Focus instead on balanced, nutritious meals. Imagine you're running a crucial software update on your computer. Would you want to interrupt it or feed it corrupted data? Of course not. Similarly, our heart needs the right 'software updates' in the form of minerals, vitamins, and other nutrients to run efficiently. Those after-work hours spent gardening or homebrewing can be complemented with fresh, heart-healthy foods from the garden or pairing that brewed beer with a nutritious, homemade meal.

Physical activity, the third pillar, doesn't necessitate grueling hours at the gym. Think about it in terms of your hobbies. Running is a fantastic cardio exercise, but it doesn't always mean training for a marathon. A brisk 30-minute walk or a light jog in the local park can do wonders. Gardening, often underrated, is an activity that involves stretching, lifting, and often, good cardiovascular work. Turning these everyday activities into regular habits can immensely benefit our heart's health.

Now, for our modern-day warriors who balance team meetings, coding sessions, and family time, managing stress is paramount. Consider stress as that one bug in your code; if not addressed, it can compromise the entire system. In the realm of heart health, chronic stress can lead to severe complications. While binge-watching a series on Netflix or Hulu might feel like the perfect de-stressor after a long day, incorporating mindfulness practices, deep-breathing exercises, or even short meditative breaks during the workday can significantly help in keeping stress levels in check.

Finally, the pillar that often gets overlooked: Sleep. Think of it as shutting down your computer after a long day. It needs to reboot, to update, to rest. For our heart, sleep plays a vital role in healing and repair. In today's fast-paced environment, where late-night emails or the allure of just one more episode can keep us awake, it's crucial to prioritize sleep.

Now, imagine blending these pillars into your daily life. Picture yourself waking up after a restful sleep, choosing a breakfast that nourishes, taking short breaks during work to breathe, and spending evenings either indulging in a hobby or with family, sharing a heart-healthy meal. This isn't a utopian vision but a reachable reality.

For the middle manager watching football during leisure time or the tech enthusiast reading the latest edition of Wired, the journey towards a heart-healthy lifestyle might seem filled with challenges. However, it's these daily choices, made with awareness and consistency, that truly make the difference. It's not about drastic changes but about informed, mindful decisions.

And as we move forward, remember: our heart, with its rhythmic beats, narrates the story of our life, of our struggles, joys, and dreams. By embracing the pillars of a heart-healthy lifestyle, we're not just adding days to our life, but life to our days. It's a journey of discovering lifelong vitality, where every beat counts.

From understanding the workings of your heart to the daily choices that make a big difference

Imagine you're at your desk, perhaps reviewing a coding project, and your heart is hard at work, as usual, beating steadily. It's like that always-on server, ensuring everything runs smoothly, rarely demanding attention. But just as any software engineer knows the intricacies of the code they write, understanding the heart's inner workings can be transformative.

At its core, the heart is a muscular pump, designed with chambers and valves, working tirelessly to send oxygen-rich blood throughout the body. Each beat is a testament to its resilience and strength, ensuring every organ, every cell gets the nourishment it needs. But beyond its physical anatomy lies a deeper understanding. The heart responds, often in real-time, to our emotions, our stress levels, our dietary choices, and physical activity.

Picture this: It's Monday morning, and an urgent email lands in your inbox. The heart rate quickens, stress hormones are released. Or, it's a weekend, and the family decides on a fast-food dinner - that extra salt, fat, and sugar have an immediate impact on blood pressure and heart load. On the flip side, a morning run or choosing a salad over fries has a positive effect, giving the heart a different kind of workout or less of a strain.

But why does this matter? For the urban-dwelling middle manager or the software engineer, life can sometimes be a series of checkboxes. Meetings attended, codes debugged, deadlines met. And in that routine, the heart's whispers can go unnoticed. Yet, understanding these signals can be the difference between proactive health choices and reactive health crises.

This brings us to daily choices. You know, those seemingly inconsequential decisions that build up over time. The latte with an extra shot of syrup, the elevator ride instead of stairs, the late-night work binge instead of restful sleep. These choices, when made consistently, can slowly steer us away from heart health.

Consider, for instance, the daily commute. For many, it involves hours of sitting. While catching up on podcasts like "The Tim Ferriss Show" or "Health Revolution" might be enlightening, the sedentary nature of the commute isn't heart-friendly. Could we perhaps park a little farther and walk? Or take short breaks during work, especially if it involves long hours at a desk?

Then there's food. In a world of convenient, processed meals and takeouts, making heart-healthy dietary choices requires a touch more effort but pays dividends. It's not just about low-fat or low-sodium, but about balanced, nutrient-rich meals. Cooking at home, especially with heart-healthy recipes, not only meets the goal of better meals but becomes a cherished family activity, a twofold win.

Beyond diet and exercise, daily choices also encompass stress management and sleep. Imagine ending a challenging workday with a session of gardening, feeling the soil, nurturing plants. It's therapeutic, grounding. Likewise, setting boundaries for work-life balance, ensuring quality sleep, and practicing mindfulness—even if it's just ten minutes a day—can substantially benefit the heart.

Another vital daily choice is continuous learning. The tech world evolves rapidly. What's groundbreaking today becomes obsolete tomorrow. Similarly, our understanding of heart health, the do's and don'ts, is ever-evolving. Platforms like Reddit, especially health forums, or apps like MyFitnessPal can be treasure troves of information, provided we approach them with discernment.

For the logical, fact-driven individual, it might be tempting to see heart health as a set of data points. Blood pressure numbers, cholesterol levels, body mass index. And while these are essential, the heart, in all its wisdom, asks for more than just data-driven care. It seeks understanding, consistency, and a touch of compassion.

As you navigate the bustling streets of the East Coast, juggling professional aspirations and family responsibilities, remember this: Every heartbeat is a story, a blend of choices made, challenges faced, and dreams chased. In this narrative, understanding the heart and making daily choices that honor its role can be the most empowering decision. Not just for longevity, but for a life lived with vitality, joy, and purpose.

Chapter 1 "A Heart's Whisper"

A brief look at what heart disease is, its potential causes, and the myriad of symptoms that can serve as early warning signals

In the heart of a bustling urban city on the East Coast, life moves at a breakneck speed. From software engineers perfecting lines of code, to middle managers juggling multiple projects, the rhythm of life is unceasing. For the 45-year-old family man, weekends may revolve around gardening, homebrewing, or cheering on a football team. Evenings might be spent unwinding with Netflix shows or an episode of "The Tim Ferriss Show." Yet, amidst this orchestra of life, there exists a silent player, often overshadowed but critically essential – the heart.

In its essence, heart disease is not merely a medical condition; it's a disruption in life's symphony. It's that glitch in the software, that unexpected challenge in project management, that unforeseen hurdle in the path of aspirations and dreams. But what is heart disease, really? At its most basic, heart disease refers to a collection of conditions affecting the heart's structure and function. This could range from issues with blood vessels, the rhythm, or even infections. And like a complex software problem, it's rarely attributable to a single cause. Instead, multiple factors interplay, some inherent, like genetics, and others a result of lifestyle choices.

Now, imagine being engrossed in debugging a challenging piece of software. You've been at it for hours, and suddenly, a series of subtle hints emerge, suggesting the problem's root. These hints, when heeded, can save hours of work, and similarly, the heart, in its profound wisdom, offers hints. Symptoms, or what could be referred to as "a heart's whispers," are early warning signals that all might not be well.

These symptoms can vary, just like bugs in different software modules. Some are overt, like chest pain or shortness of breath. Others are subtle, perhaps an unexplained fatigue or a slight pain in the arm or jaw. For the logical, fact-driven individual, these signals could seem minor, easy to brush aside in the pursuit of daily goals. But in the grander narrative of life and wellness, acknowledging these whispers can be paramount.

As you weave through the urban streets, perhaps contemplating the next tech conference or planning a health retreat, consider the factors that contribute to heart disease. The saturated fats from that fast-food burger, the additional stress of tight deadlines, or even the genetic history of heart conditions in the family; they all play a role. The excessive sodium in processed foods, the sedentary hours spent in front of screens, and even exposure to prolonged high levels of stress, each contribute to the heart disease tapestry.

However, amidst this somewhat somber reflection, there lies hope, for the heart is resilient. It's that reliable code running in the background, and with care, its efficiency can be optimized. By understanding heart disease, its causes, and its symptoms, one can pivot, making choices that enhance heart health. It's like refining the code, optimizing processes, ensuring that the system runs seamlessly.

For the avid runner, or even the occasional video game enthusiast, integrating heart-healthy choices becomes an engaging challenge. It's about choosing stairs over elevators, opting for fresh produce over processed snacks, and dedicating time to mindfulness and relaxation. It's about viewing heart health not as a chore but as a project, one that promises rich dividends in the form of vitality and longevity.

But remember, in the realm of heart health, it's not just about individual choices. It's a collective endeavor. Cooking heart-healthy meals becomes not just a personal goal but a familial activity. It's about teaching kids the value of balanced nutrition and the joy of culinary experiments. It's about sharing with a spouse the findings from a Reddit health forum or a revelation from a "Health Revolution" episode. It's a journey, one that's enriched when shared with loved ones.

As you delve into books like Men's Health or Wired, as you engage in emails, prioritizing facts and summaries, let heart health be a consistent theme, subtly integrated into daily life. Let it be the background music to family dinners, the topic of discussion during a run, or even the inspiration for a homebrewing session. For in understanding heart disease, its causes, and its symptoms, lies the power to rewrite life's script. A script where heart health isn't a mere chapter but the very essence of the narrative.

In the grand tapestry of life, heart whispers might seem faint, easy to overlook amidst louder calls. But for the discerning, for those tuned in, these whispers offer a chance, an opportunity to refine, to optimize, and to cherish the heart's relentless service. So, as you navigate the challenges and joys of urban life on the East Coast, pause, listen, and heed the heart's whisper. It's a dialogue, one that promises health, happiness, and a harmony that resonates with life's every beat.

Understand why it's essential to give heed to these signals and take proactive measures

In the shimmering metropolis of the East Coast, amid the ever-present hum of ambition and progress, there's an innate human tendency to focus on what's immediately before us. The next email in our inbox, the next meeting on our calendar, the next challenge to troubleshoot. But sometimes, in this relentless pursuit of the next big thing, we tend to overlook the subtle signs our body offers us. These signs, these gentle nudges, particularly from our heart, are our body's way of seeking attention. They are a form of communication, as intrinsic as the emails we prioritize or the discussions we have with our teams. And just as in the realm of work and family, in the intricate dance of health, these signals bear significant importance.

Picture this: you're overseeing a critical project, and a team member offers a minor observation. It's easy to overlook it in the larger scheme of things, right? But often, it's these minor observations, when heeded, that prevent bigger complications down the line. Similarly, our heart, that diligent worker operating in the background of our existence, occasionally sends out signals, its own observations. Ignoring them might seem harmless initially, but in the long run, it can escalate into larger, more severe complications.

Consider the quiet moments post a hectic day, when you're in your urban sanctuary, perhaps sipping on a homebrew or planning the plants for your garden. It's in these quiet moments that the heart's whispers are most audible. A slight discomfort here, a fleeting pain there, or perhaps an unexplained fatigue. For someone driven by facts, by logic, it's tempting to attribute these symptoms to the rigors of daily life. But therein lies the crux. Our heart doesn't whisper without reason. These are not random occurrences but calculated alerts.

Now, let's relate this to something more tangible. Imagine you're debugging a software issue. The system keeps flagging a minor glitch. You can choose to bypass it, considering it insignificant. But experienced engineers know that minor glitches can be precursors to system-wide crashes. Similarly, those seemingly insignificant heart symptoms? They can be precursors to conditions that are not just debilitating but can redefine the very essence of our existence.

Giving heed to these signals is not about fear; it's about respect. Respect for one's body, respect for the intricate machinery that allows us to chase our dreams, to enjoy the leisure of a football game, or the thrill of running. And respecting these signals means taking proactive measures.

Being proactive is a concept we're all familiar with, especially in the corporate world. It's about anticipating challenges and addressing them before they become issues. When applied to heart health, it means acknowledging the heart's whispers and taking actionable steps. This could be as simple as scheduling a routine check-up, adjusting dietary choices, or even re-evaluating exercise regimes.

Imagine, after a day's work, as you indulge in the latest show on Netflix or dive into a discussion on Reddit's health forum, you come across heart-healthy tips. It's easy to bypass, right? But integrating them, making them a part of your daily routine, can be as fulfilling as acing a project at work. It's about viewing heart health not as an obligation but as a project, one with immense personal ROI.

And these proactive measures, they don't operate in isolation. They become a collective endeavor. It's about sharing a heart-healthy recipe with the family, making meal times not just about nourishment but about wellness. It's about integrating short breaks into your work routine, ensuring that while you chase professional excellence, you're not sidelining your health.

The pursuit of heart health is akin to the software projects that define careers. It's about iterations, constant refinements. And just as in software, where periodic updates prevent glitches, in the realm of health, periodic check-ups and lifestyle adjustments prevent complications.

To further draw upon this idea, let's consider the games we treasure, the ones that offer moments of respite from the daily grind. Whether it's the calculated strategy of a video game or the highs and lows of a football match, every game has its signals, its moments of decision. In football, a quarterback reads the defense, looks for signals, and makes the split-second decision that could lead to a game-winning touchdown. The same holds true for our health. Reading and acting upon the early signals can lead to victories, albeit of a different kind – victories over potential health challenges, ensuring longevity and vitality.

Moreover, for our audience who thrives in a data-driven, tech-savvy environment, the concept of monitoring and metrics is nothing new. Just as we would never ignore an important email or bypass a critical software update, why should we treat our body's signals with any less urgency? Think of these signals as timely notifications, nudging you to act, to refine, to iterate. We live in an age of wearable tech, apps, and platforms that can help us monitor our health metrics seamlessly. A resting heart rate, blood pressure, or cholesterol level might seem like mere numbers, but in reality, they are data points – indicators of the state of our most crucial organ.

Many might argue, with demanding careers and familial responsibilities, how can one possibly prioritize these signals? But that's the beauty of it; understanding and acting upon these signals doesn't require monumental shifts. It's about small, consistent, and informed choices. A choice to opt for a salad over a burger, a decision to take the stairs over the elevator, or a commitment to a 10-minute daily meditation routine to manage stress.

For someone whose leisure might be intricately tied with the digital world, platforms like MyFitnessPal or WebMD aren't just apps; they can be allies. They offer a reservoir of information, help track progress, and more importantly, make the journey towards heart health interactive and engaging.

While influencers like Joe Rogan or Tim Ferriss provide insights into myriad subjects, it's worth delving into their takes on health and wellness. Their interviews with cardiologists, nutritionists, and fitness experts can offer not just knowledge but actionable advice. These aren't mere podcasts; they can be classrooms, offering lessons in heart health, urging listeners to not just hear but to listen, to internalize, and to act.

But this journey, as logical and data-driven as it might be, is also deeply personal. It's about rediscovering a connection with oneself, understanding the nuances of one's body, and nurturing it. It's about cherishing moments with loved ones, ensuring that every family meal, every holiday, every milestone is underscored by the rhythm of a healthy heart.

In the end, heart health isn't just a physical pursuit; it's an emotional and intellectual one too. It's a commitment to oneself, a promise to honor the heart's whispers. For in these whispers lies wisdom, a wisdom that urges us to be proactive, to cherish the present, and to build a future where every heartbeat resonates with joy, vitality, and unwavering purpose.

Chapter 2 "For a Heart That Beats Strong"

Learn about the role of diet in heart health

When the hum of a bustling urban city fades each evening, when the glow of monitors dims and emails no longer ping, there's one rhythm that remains — the heartbeat. It's a steady, reassuring reminder of life itself. The quest to keep this rhythm going strong isn't just about cardiovascular exercises or routine check-ups. It's intricately linked to what we consume, how we fuel our bodies. The old adage, "You are what you eat," holds profound wisdom, especially when it comes to our heart's well-being.

Picture this: You've just wrapped up a long day at the tech firm. As you disconnect from the digital world, your thoughts drift to dinner. Now, imagine if that meal, besides being a source of relaxation and nourishment, could also be a shield, a protective barrier for your heart.

It's often easy to dismiss the role of diet in heart health. After all, we live in times where convenience is prized, where takeaway meals are just a click away, and where snacks come in packages, promising instant gratification. But dig deeper, and it becomes evident that the food choices we make have profound implications for our heart's health.

You might wonder, what does it mean to eat for a heart that beats strong? Is it about strict diets, grim restrictions, or giving up on flavors? Thankfully, no. It's about understanding, choosing, and embracing foods that not only satiate our palates but also nurture our hearts.

For instance, there's a world of difference between a meal laden with trans fats, sugars, and excessive salt and a meal rich in omega-3 fatty acids, fiber, and antioxidants. The former, often found in processed foods, can lead to cholesterol build-up, hypertension, and inflammation — all adversaries of a healthy heart. The latter, abundantly present in foods like fatty fish, nuts, whole grains, and a plethora of fruits and vegetables, are allies, ensuring smooth blood flow, reduced inflammation, and overall heart vitality.

But how does one navigate this dietary maze, especially when bombarded with an overload of information? For our logical, fact-driven reader, it's not about blindly following diet fads. It's about informed choices. Dive deep into credible sources, be it WebMD, health-focused Reddit threads, or the health segment in Men's Health magazine. Listen to experts on "The Tim Ferriss Show" or "Health Revolution" podcasts. These platforms aren't just for passive consumption; they can guide, inspire, and offer actionable insights.

Let's say you're passionate about homebrewing. Now, moderate alcohol consumption, especially red wine, has been linked to certain heart benefits. But the keyword here is 'moderate.' Just like the precision required in brewing, there's precision in consumption, ensuring it's beneficial and not detrimental.

Or consider gardening, another hobby that many cherish. Beyond its therapeutic joys, gardening can be a source of heart-healthy foods. Fresh produce, be it tomatoes bursting with antioxidants or leafy greens rich in vitamins, can be pivotal in crafting meals that are not just delicious but heart-boosting.

Speaking of meals, there's a misconception that heart-healthy cooking is a complex, time-consuming affair. But delve into it, and you'll realize it's an art, one that's accessible and deeply rewarding. Swapping refined grains for whole ones, choosing lean proteins, reducing sodium, and incorporating a rainbow of fruits and vegetables doesn't just make for a heart-healthy meal; it's a sensory delight, a dance of textures and flavors.

As you evolve in your culinary journey, perhaps even learning from platforms like MyFitnessPal, you'll realize that every meal, every snack is an opportunity. An opportunity to fortify, to heal, to rejuvenate. And the beauty of it all is that it's not a solo journey. Cooking and sharing heart-healthy meals can be a family affair, a way to ensure that the heartbeats of those you hold dear remain strong and vibrant.

In conclusion, the heart, with its rhythmic beats, is a marvel, a testament to life's resilience and beauty. And just like any marvel, it deserves care, attention, and respect. As we navigate the intricate tapestry of life, juggling professional commitments, personal passions, and familial ties, let's not forget the role of diet in ensuring our heart's well-being. It's not just about adding years to life but adding life to those years, ensuring that every heartbeat resonates with strength, vitality, and unyielding joy.

Discover the therapeutic power of heart-healthy foods, the art of choosing them, and how to make them part of your everyday meals

Life is a series of rhythms and routines, punctuated by choices that carry profound implications. One such choice revolves around the food we place on our plates, and more specifically, how these foods become instruments of therapy, especially for our hearts. For in food lies power, a therapeutic power, one that can shield, heal, and rejuvenate our cardiovascular system.

Imagine coming home after a long, exhausting day at the tech firm, having maneuvered through complex software codes and intricate managerial decisions. As you shed the weight of your responsibilities, you are greeted with the comforting aroma of a home-cooked meal — one that's not just delightful to the senses but also brimming with heart-healthy goodness. It's more than just a meal; it's medicine in its most delicious form.

So, what makes certain foods therapeutic for the heart? It's their rich profile of nutrients that actively combat the enemies of heart health. Foods rich in omega-3 fatty acids, like salmon and walnuts, work wonders in reducing inflammation, a key factor in cardiovascular diseases. Berries, with their vibrant colors and flavors, bring with them a host of antioxidants that fight oxidative stress. The fiber from whole grains ensures smooth digestion and helps maintain cholesterol levels.

But knowing about these heart-healthy foods is just the beginning. The real art lies in choosing them consciously and integrating them seamlessly into our daily meals. For our fact-driven, logical reader, this isn't about whims or fancies; it's a calculated, informed decision — a commitment to the heart.

Choosing heart-healthy foods begins at the grocery store. Navigating the aisles can be overwhelming, given the plethora of options. But with a discerning eye, one can spot the treasures. Opt for fresh produce over canned or processed versions. The aisles are more than just shelves of commodities; they are galleries showcasing nature's therapeutic wonders. Here's where knowledge, gathered from trusted sources like WebMD or Men's Health, can be a beacon, guiding one towards choices that resonate with health.

But selection is only half the battle. The next challenge is making these foods a staple in everyday meals. This is where creativity and passion intertwine. Think of your kitchen as a canvas, where heart-healthy foods become the colors with which you paint.

Let's delve into the realm of imagination. Picture a hearty salad, where crisp leafy greens are adorned with slices of avocados, rich in monounsaturated fats, and sprinkled with chia seeds, a powerhouse of omega-3s. Or visualize a comforting bowl of oatmeal, elevated with a handful of blueberries and a drizzle of honey. The possibilities are endless, limited only by one's creativity.

And as you embark on this culinary journey, you'll discover the joy of sharing. After all, heart health isn't a solitary quest. It's a journey best undertaken with loved ones. Picture a weekend, where the family comes together, laughing, bonding, and cooking. Children, with their infectious enthusiasm, can be the sous-chefs, washing and prepping vegetables. Your partner, perhaps, takes on the role of the chef, weaving magic with flavors and textures. And as the family sits down to dine, there's a shared sense of accomplishment — a meal that's not just about satiating hunger but about nurturing the heart.

Integrating heart-healthy foods into meals also opens doors to exploration. The world of culinary arts is vast, with each culture bringing its palette of flavors and health benefits. For instance, the Mediterranean diet, with its emphasis on fresh produce, whole grains, and healthy fats, has been lauded for its cardiovascular benefits. Or consider the Japanese diet, where portions are controlled, and there's a harmonious balance of nutrients. Exploring these cuisines can be an adventurous journey, one that tantalizes the taste buds while fortifying the heart.

In conclusion, the heart, that magnificent organ that tirelessly pumps life through our veins, deserves nothing but the best. And in the realm of food lies the power to bestow upon it the care it warrants. As days morph into nights, as professional challenges give way to personal joys, let's pledge to embrace the therapeutic power of heart-healthy foods. Let's master the art of choosing them, making them an indelible part of our meals, our routines. For in this commitment lies the promise of a heart that beats strong, a life that resonates with vibrancy and vigor.

Chapter 3 "Palette of Heart Wellness"

Breakfast

Sunlit Spinach Scramble

Time: 15 minutes

Ingredients:

2 cups fresh spinach, chopped

4 large eggs

1 ripe avocado, diced

1/4 cup walnuts, chopped

Servings: 3

Method: Whisk eggs, fold in chopped spinach and diced avocado, cook on low heat until set.

Nutrition: 200 calories; 15g fat; 5g carbs; 12g protein

Blueberry Bliss Bowl

Time: 10 minutes

Ingredients:

1 cup blueberries

1 cup Greek yogurt

1/4 cup almonds, crushed

Servings: 2

Method: Mix blueberries with yogurt, top with crushed almonds.

Nutrition: 150 calories; 7g fat; 17g carbs; 8g protein

Quinoa Quietude Quiche

Time: 40 minutes

Ingredients:

1 cup cooked quinoa

2 cups fresh spinach, chopped

1/2 cup feta cheese, crumbled

4 large eggs, beaten

Servings: 4

Method: Layer quinoa, spinach, feta, pour whisked eggs, and bake.

Nutrition: 220 calories; 12g fat; 18g carbs; 10g protein

Oat's Ocean Odyssey

Time: Overnight (15 minutes prep)

Ingredients:

1 cup rolled oats

2 cups almond milk

2 tablespoons chia seeds

2 tablespoons maple syrup

Servings: 2

Method: Mix ingredients, let soak overnight.

Nutrition: 180 calories; 8g fat; 25g carbs; 6g protein

Tropical Tranquility Toast

Time: 10 minutes

Ingredients:

2 slices of whole-grain bread

1 ripe avocado

1 ripe mango, sliced

1 tablespoon honey

Servings: 2

Method: Toast bread, spread avocado, add mango slices, drizzle honey.

Nutrition: 210 calories; 9g fat; 30g carbs; 6g protein

Walnut Wonder Waffles

Time: 20 minutes

Ingredients:

1 cup walnuts

2 ripe bananas

4 large eggs

1 teaspoon cinnamon

Servings: 3

Method: Blend ingredients, cook in waffle iron.

Nutrition: 250 calories; 15g fat; 24g carbs; 8g protein

Peachy Plateau Porridge

Time: 20 minutes

Ingredients:

2 peaches, sliced

1 cup rolled oats

2 tablespoons honey

2 cups almond milk

Servings: 3

Method: Cook oats in milk, add peaches and honey.

Nutrition: 190 calories; 4g fat; 35g carbs; 5g protein

Raspberry Reverie Rolls

Time: 25 minutes

Ingredients:

1 cup raspberries

3 whole wheat wraps

1/2 cup cream cheese

Zest of 1 lemon

Servings: 3

Method: Spread cheese on wraps, add raspberries, lemon zest, roll.

Nutrition: 210 calories; 9g fat; 29g carbs; 7g protein

Kiwi's Kindred Kale Smoothie

Time: 10 minutes

Ingredients:

2 ripe kiwis, peeled

1 cup chopped kale

1 ripe banana

2 cups almond milk

Servings: 2

Method: Blend all ingredients until smooth.

Nutrition: 180 calories; 3g fat; 40g carbs; 5g protein

Chia's Celestial Cereal

Time: 10 minutes

Ingredients:

1/4 cup chia seeds

1/4 cup almonds, chopped

2 cups coconut milk

2 tablespoons date syrup

Servings: 3

Method: Soak chia seeds in milk, top with almonds, date syrup.

Nutrition: 220 calories; 14g fat; 20g carbs; 7g protein

Cucumber's Calm Crêpes

Time: 25 minutes

Ingredients:

1 large cucumber, thinly sliced

1 cup whole wheat flour

1/2 cup feta cheese, crumbled

Zest of 1 lemon

Servings: 3

Method: Make crêpes, fill with cucumber, feta, lemon zest.

Nutrition: 210 calories; 8g fat; 28g carbs; 9g protein

Apple's Aura Acai Bowl

Time: 15 minutes

Ingredients:

1 apple, chopped

2 packets frozen acai puree

1/2 cup granola

2 tablespoons honey

Servings: 2

Method: Blend acai and apple, top with granola, honey.

Nutrition: 270 calories; 6g fat; 50g carbs; 5g protein

Tofu's Twilight Toasties

Time: 20 minutes

Ingredients:

1 block firm tofu, sliced

2 tomatoes, sliced

Fresh basil leaves

Olive oil for drizzling

Servings: 3

Method: Grill tofu, top with tomato, basil, olive oil.

Nutrition: 190 calories; 9g fat; 10g carbs; 14g protein

Pineapple's Peaceful Pancakes

Time: 30 minutes

Ingredients:

1 cup chopped pineapple

1 cup almond flour

4 large eggs

Shredded coconut for topping

Servings: 3

Method: Mix flour, eggs, pineapple, cook on griddle.

Nutrition: 240 calories; 15g fat; 20g carbs; 10g protein

Strawberry's Stillness Scones

Time: 40 minutes

Ingredients:

1 cup diced strawberries

2 cups oat flour

1 cup yogurt

2 tablespoons maple syrup

Servings: 4

Method: Combine ingredients, shape into scones, bake.

Nutrition: 210 calories; 3g fat; 40g carbs; 7g protein

Fig's Forest Farina

Time: 20 minutes

Ingredients:

5 figs, chopped

1 cup farina (cream of wheat)

2 cups almond milk

1 teaspoon cinnamon

Servings: 2

Method: Cook farina in milk, add figs, cinnamon.

Nutrition: 220 calories; 4g fat; 45g carbs; 5g protein

Blackberry's Breeze Bagels

Time: 30 minutes

Ingredients:

1 cup blackberries

3 whole wheat bagels, halved

1/2 cup cream cheese

2 tablespoons chia seeds

Servings: 3

Method: Spread cheese on bagels, top with blackberries, chia seeds.

Nutrition: 270 calories; 9g fat; 42g carbs; 10g protein

Orange's Oasis Overnight Oats

Time: Overnight (10 minutes prep)

Ingredients:

Zest of 1 orange

1 cup rolled oats

1 cup yogurt

2 tablespoons honey

Servings: 2

Method: Mix ingredients, refrigerate overnight.

Nutrition: 230 calories; 4g fat; 45g carbs; 8g protein

Plum's Prelude Pudding

Time: 20 minutes

Ingredients:

4 plums, chopped

1/4 cup chia seeds

2 cups coconut milk

1 teaspoon vanilla extract

Servings: 3

Method: Mix ingredients, let soak until thickened.

Nutrition: 220 calories; 12g fat; 25g carbs; 6g protein

Banana's Beachside Burrito

Time: 25 minutes

Ingredients:

3 bananas, sliced

3 whole wheat wraps

1/4 cup almond butter

1/4 cup coconut shreds

Servings: 3

Method: Spread butter on wraps, add banana, coconut, roll.

Nutrition: 310 calories; 15g fat; 40g carbs; 9g protein

Sides & Salads

Cherry's Chorus Coleslaw

Time: 15 minutes

Ingredients:

2 cups cherries, pitted and halved

4 cups cabbage, shredded

2 carrots, grated

1/4 cup vinegar

Servings: 4

Method: Combine shredded cabbage, grated carrots, halved cherries, and vinegar.

Nutrition: 60 calories; 0g fat; 15g carbs; 2g protein

Pumpkin's Pastoral Potato Salad

Time: 25 minutes

Ingredients:

2 cups pumpkin, diced

4 medium potatoes, cubed

1/4 cup green onions, chopped

2 tablespoons mustard

Servings: 5

Method: Boil cubed potatoes, mix with diced pumpkin, green onions, mustard.

Nutrition: 140 calories; 1g fat; 30g carbs; 4g protein

Cilantro's Symphony Spinach Salad

Time: 10 minutes

Ingredients:

3 cups spinach leaves

1/2 cup cilantro, chopped

1/2 cup feta cheese, crumbled

Juice of 1 lemon

Servings: 3

Method: Arrange spinach, feta, cilantro, and sprinkle with lemon juice.

Nutrition: 90 calories; 5g fat; 8g carbs; 5g protein

Tomato's Tango Tabbouleh

Time: 20 minutes

Ingredients:

2 cups tomatoes, diced

1 cup bulgur wheat, soaked and drained

1 cup parsley, chopped

2 tablespoons olive oil

Servings: 4

Method: Combine soaked bulgur, diced tomatoes, chopped parsley, olive oil.

Nutrition: 170 calories; 7g fat; 25g carbs; 5g protein

Asparagus's Adagio Aioli

Time: 20 minutes

Ingredients:

1 bunch asparagus

2 cloves garlic

1/2 cup yogurt

Juice of 1 lemon

Servings: 3

Method: Sauté asparagus, blend garlic, yogurt, lemon for aioli, serve together.

Nutrition: 80 calories; 1g fat; 15g carbs; 5g protein

Radish's Rhapsody Rice Salad

Time: 25 minutes

Ingredients:

1 cup radishes, thinly sliced

2 cups cooked rice

1 cucumber, diced

2 tablespoons vinegar

Servings: 4

Method: Combine cooked rice, sliced radishes, diced cucumber, and vinegar.

Nutrition: 180 calories; 1g fat; 37g carbs; 4g protein

Beet's Ballet Bean Salad

Time: 20 minutes

Ingredients:

2 cups beets, roasted and diced

2 cups cooked beans

1 cup corn, steamed

1 teaspoon fresh thyme

Servings: 5

Method: Mix cooked beans, roasted beets, steamed corn, season with thyme.

Nutrition: 160 calories; 1g fat; 34g carbs; 8g protein

Mango's Minuet Millet Salad

Time: 30 minutes

Ingredients:

1 mango, diced

2 cups cooked millet

1 red pepper, diced

Juice of 1 lime

Servings: 4

Method: Fluff cooked millet, add diced mango, red pepper, lime juice.

Nutrition: 210 calories; 2g fat; 45g carbs; 6g protein

Pear's Polonaise Parsnip Purée

Time: 40 minutes

Ingredients:

2 pears, peeled and chopped

4 parsnips, peeled and chopped

1 cup almond milk

1/4 teaspoon nutmeg

Servings: 3

Method: Steam pears, parsnips, blend with almond milk, season with nutmeg.

Nutrition: 150 calories; 1g fat; 35g carbs; 3g protein

Olive's Overture Orzo Salad

Time: 25 minutes

Ingredients:

1 cup olives, sliced

2 cups cooked orzo

1/2 cup feta cheese, crumbled

1/4 cup fresh basil, torn

Servings: 5

Method: Mix cooked orzo, sliced olives, crumbled feta, torn basil.

Nutrition: 230 calories; 8g fat; 32g carbs; 8g protein

Zucchini's Zen Zest Salad

Time: 15 minutes

Ingredients:

2 zucchinis, spiralized

1/4 cup almonds, sliced

1/4 cup dried cranberries

1 tablespoon fresh mint, chopped

Servings: 4

Method: Spiralize zucchini, combine with almonds, cranberries, mint.

Nutrition: 95 calories; 4g fat; 14g carbs; 3g protein

Sweet Potato's Sonnet Slaw

Time: 20 minutes

Ingredients:

2 sweet potatoes, grated

2 apples, grated

1/2 cup raisins

1 teaspoon cinnamon

Servings: 5

Method: Grate sweet potatoes, apples, mix with raisins, cinnamon.

Nutrition: 110 calories; 0.5g fat; 26g carbs; 2g protein

Broccoli's Ballad Brussels Sprouts

Time: 25 minutes

Ingredients:

2 cups broccoli, chopped

2 cups Brussels sprouts, halved

1/2 cup pecans

2 tablespoons maple syrup

Servings: 4

Method: Roast broccoli, Brussels sprouts, toss with pecans, maple syrup.

Nutrition: 135 calories; 8g fat; 16g carbs; 5g protein

Corn's Cantata Couscous Salad

Time: 20 minutes

Ingredients:

1 cup corn kernels

2 cups cooked couscous

1 can black beans, drained

1 avocado, diced

Servings: 4

Method: Mix cooked couscous, corn, black beans, diced avocado.

Nutrition: 220 calories; 7g fat; 37g carbs; 7g protein

Cauliflower's Concerto Caprese

Time: 20 minutes

Ingredients:

1 head cauliflower, sliced

2 tomatoes, sliced

1/2 cup fresh basil leaves

1 ball fresh mozzarella, sliced

Servings: 5

Method: Layer cauliflower, tomatoes, mozzarella, basil.

Nutrition: 155 calories; 9g fat; 10g carbs; 10g protein

Eggplant's Elegy Edamame

Time: 30 minutes

Ingredients:

2 eggplants, sliced

1 cup edamame

2 tablespoons tahini

1 tablespoon sesame seeds

Servings: 4

Method: Roast eggplant, mix with edamame, tahini, sprinkle sesame seeds.

Nutrition: 190 calories; 11g fat; 16g carbs; 9g protein

Cabbage's Cantabile Carrot Mix

Time: 15 minutes

Ingredients:

4 cups cabbage, shredded

2 carrots, grated

1/2 cup peanuts

2 tablespoons soy sauce

Servings: 5

Method: Toss shredded cabbage, carrots, peanuts, soy sauce.

Nutrition: 125 calories; 6g fat; 15g carbs; 5g protein

Quinoa's Quartet Quiche

Time: 40 minutes

Ingredients:

1 cup cooked quinoa

2 cups spinach, chopped

1/2 cup feta cheese, crumbled

4 large eggs, beaten

Servings: 6

Method: Press quinoa as crust, layer spinach, feta, eggs, bake.

Nutrition: 210 calories; 10g fat; 20g carbs; 11g protein

Lentil's Lullaby Lettuce Wrap

Time: 25 minutes

Ingredients:

2 cups cooked lentils

8 lettuce leaves

1 bell pepper, diced

1 teaspoon cumin

Servings: 4

Method: Mix lentils, bell peppers, cumin, serve in lettuce leaves.

Nutrition: 180 calories; 1g fat; 32g carbs; 13g protein

Artichoke's Anthem Avocado Dip

Time: 20 minutes

Ingredients:

1 cup artichoke hearts

1 ripe avocado

Juice of 1 lemon

1 clove garlic, minced

Servings: 4

Method: Blend artichokes, avocado, lemon juice, garlic.

Nutrition: 230 calories; 20g fat; 12g carbs; 4g protein

Main Cours (Meat & Poultry)

Chicken Curry

Time: 45 minutes

Ingredients:

1 1/2 pounds chicken breast, cut into cubes

2 cups tomatoes, diced

2 tablespoons ginger, minced

1 can (14 oz) coconut milk

Servings: 4

Method: Sauté chicken, add ginger, tomatoes, simmer in coconut milk until tender.

Nutrition: 310 calories; 18g fat; 8g carbs; 32g protein

Beef Bourguignon

Time: 3 hours

Ingredients:

2 pounds beef chuck, cut into cubes

3 cups red wine

2 onions, chopped

2 tablespoons fresh thyme, chopped

Servings: 6

Method: Slow-cook beef with red wine, onions, and thyme until tender.

Nutrition: 440 calories; 20g fat; 10g carbs; 45g protein

Pork Pancetta Wraps

Time: 35 minutes

Ingredients:

4 pork tenderloins

8 slices pancetta

2 tablespoons fresh sage, chopped

1 apple, sliced

Servings: 4

Method: Wrap pork in pancetta, sear, roast, and serve with apple-sage sauce.

Nutrition: 390 calories; 25g fat; 9g carbs; 32g protein

Turkey Tagine

Time: 1 hour

Ingredients:

2 pounds turkey breast, cubed

1 cup dried apricots, chopped

1/2 cup almonds, slivered

1 teaspoon saffron threads

Servings: 5

Method: Slow-cook turkey with apricots, almonds, saffron in a tagine.

Nutrition: 335 calories; 12g fat; 22g carbs; 37g protein

Duck with Damson Sauce

Time: 50 minutes

Ingredients:

4 duck breasts

1 cup damson plums, pitted and chopped

2 sprigs rosemary

1 cup red wine

Servings: 4

Method: Sear duck, simmer with damson, rosemary, red wine reduction.

Nutrition: 410 calories; 24g fat; 15g carbs; 30g protein

Lamb with Lentils

Time: 1 hour

Ingredients:

2 pounds lamb shoulder, cubed

2 cups lentils

2 carrots, diced

1/4 cup fresh mint, chopped

Servings: 4

Method: Braise lamb with lentils, carrots, finish with mint.

Nutrition: 450 calories; 23g fat; 27g carbs; 35g protein

Veal with Vegetables

Time: 45 minutes

Ingredients:

4 veal steaks

2 bell peppers, sliced

2 zucchinis, sliced

1/4 cup fresh basil, chopped

Servings: 4

Method: Pan-sear veal, sauté with peppers, zucchini, basil.

Nutrition: 320 calories; 15g fat; 10g carbs; 37g protein

Bison with Blueberry Sauce

Time: 1 hour

Ingredients:

4 bison steaks

1 cup blueberries

2 tablespoons fresh thyme

2 tablespoons maple syrup

Servings: 4

Method: Sear bison, simmer with blueberries, thyme, maple.

Nutrition: 370 calories; 20g fat; 20g carbs; 30g protein

Rabbit Stew with Rosemary

Time: 1.5 hours

Ingredients:

1 whole rabbit, cut into pieces

4 potatoes, cubed

2 sprigs rosemary

1 cup white wine

Servings: 4

Method: Slow-cook rabbit with potatoes, rosemary, and wine.

Nutrition: 340 calories; 10g fat; 23g carbs; 38g protein

Quail with Quinoa

Time: 40 minutes

Ingredients:

4 quails

2 cups cooked quinoa

1 cup pomegranate seeds

1/2 cup olives, sliced

Servings: 4

Method: Roast quails, serve on quinoa with pomegranate, olives.

Nutrition: 290 calories; 13g fat; 22g carbs; 24g protein

Partridge Pie

Time: 1 hour

Ingredients:

4 partridges, deboned and diced

4 potatoes, mashed

2 leeks, sliced

2 tablespoons fresh rosemary, chopped

Servings: 4

Method: Braise partridge with leeks, top with mashed potato, rosemary, bake.

Nutrition: 320 calories; 12g fat; 28g carbs; 25g protein

Sirloin with Shallots

Time: 45 minutes

Ingredients:

4 sirloin steaks

1 cup shallots, sliced

2 cloves garlic, minced

1 cup red wine

Servings: 4

Method: Sear steaks, sauté shallots, garlic, deglaze with wine.

Nutrition: 435 calories; 28g fat; 6g carbs; 35g protein

Cornish Hen with Herbs

Time: 1 hour

Ingredients:

4 Cornish hens

2 tablespoons fresh sage, chopped

2 tablespoons fresh parsley, chopped

Zest of 2 lemons

Servings: 4

Method: Steam hens with herbs, finish with lemon zest.

Nutrition: 275 calories; 14g fat; 3g carbs; 32g protein

Osso Bucco

Time: 3 hours

Ingredients:

4 beef shanks

2 cups tomatoes, crushed

2 carrots, diced

2 bay leaves

Servings: 6

Method: Braise beef shanks in tomato sauce with vegetables, bay leaves.

Nutrition: 500 calories; 25g fat; 18g carbs; 45g protein

Sausage with Spinach

Time: 40 minutes

Ingredients:

5 sausages

2 cups spinach, chopped

2 cloves garlic, minced

1/4 teaspoon nutmeg

Servings: 5

Method: Brown sausages, add spinach, garlic, finish with nutmeg.

Nutrition: 380 calories; 28g fat; 5g carbs; 28g protein

Ribs with Rosemary

Time: 3 hours

Ingredients:

2 racks ribs

2 tablespoons fresh rosemary, chopped

1 onion, chopped

2 cups apple cider

Servings: 4

Method: Slow-cook ribs with rosemary, onion, apple cider.

Nutrition: 520 calories; 35g fat; 12g carbs; 40g protein

Mutton with Mushrooms

Time: 2 hours

Ingredients:

2 pounds mutton, cut into cubes

2 cups mushrooms, sliced

2 tablespoons fresh thyme

1 cup red wine

Servings: 4

Method: Slow-cook mutton with mushrooms, thyme, and wine.

Nutrition: 460 calories; 24g fat; 10g carbs; 48g protein

Game Hen with Grapes

Time: 1 hour

Ingredients:

4 game hens

1 cup grapes, halved

2 tablespoons fresh tarragon, chopped

2 tablespoons honey

Servings: 4

Method: Roast hens, serve with grape, tarragon, honey sauce.

Nutrition: 310 calories; 15g fat; 18g carbs; 30g protein

Pheasant with Plums

Time: 1.5 hours

Ingredients:

4 pheasants, cut into pieces

2 cups plums, pitted and sliced

1 tablespoon juniper berries

1/2 cup brandy

Servings: 4

Method: Braise pheasant with plums, juniper, brandy.

Nutrition: 350 calories; 12g fat; 22g carbs; 38g protein

Venison with Vegetables

Time: 2 hours

Ingredients:

2 pounds venison, cubed

2 carrots, diced

2 stalks celery, diced

1 teaspoon cloves

Servings: 4

Method: Slow-cook venison in vegetable broth with cloves.

Nutrition: 340 calories; 15g fat; 15g carbs; 40g protein

Seafood Delights

Salmon with Sage

Time: 25 minutes

Ingredients:

4 salmon fillets (about 6 oz each)

2 tablespoons fresh sage, chopped

Zest of 1 lemon

2 tablespoons olive oil

Servings: 4

Method: Pan-sear salmon with sage and lemon zest, finish with olive oil.

Nutrition: 260 calories; 12g fat; 0g carbs; 35g protein

Tuna with Tarragon

Time: 20 minutes

Ingredients:

4 tuna steaks (about 6 oz each)

2 tablespoons fresh tarragon, chopped

1/2 cup white wine

2 cloves garlic, minced

Servings: 4

Method: Sauté tuna with tarragon and garlic, deglaze with white wine.

Nutrition: 240 calories; 6g fat; 1g carbs; 40g protein

Shrimp Sauté with Tequila

Time: 15 minutes

Ingredients:

1 pound shrimp, peeled and deveined

1 teaspoon paprika

Juice of 1 lime

2 tablespoons tequila

Servings: 4

Method: Sauté shrimp with paprika and lime, add a splash of tequila.

Nutrition: 170 calories; 2g fat; 2g carbs; 33g protein

Cod with Capers

Time: 25 minutes

Ingredients:

4 cod fillets (about 6 oz each)

2 tablespoons capers

Juice of 1 lemon

2 tablespoons fresh dill, chopped

Servings: 4

Method: Bake cod with lemon, dill, and capers.

Nutrition: 190 calories; 1g fat; 2g carbs; 40g protein

Mussels with Mint

Time: 20 minutes

Ingredients:

2 pounds mussels, cleaned

1/4 cup fresh mint, chopped

1 cup coconut milk

1 teaspoon chili flakes

Servings: 2

Method: Steam mussels in coconut milk with mint and chili.

Nutrition: 300 calories; 14g fat; 10g carbs; 30g protein

Lobster in Lemon Butter

Time: 40 minutes

Ingredients:

2 whole lobsters

1/4 cup butter, melted

Juice of 1 lemon

2 tablespoons fresh parsley, chopped

Servings: 2

Method: Steam lobster, serve with lemon butter sauce, garnish with parsley.

Nutrition: 350 calories; 25g fat; 2g carbs; 30g protein

Clams with Cilantro

Time: 20 minutes

Ingredients:

2 pounds clams, cleaned

1/4 cup fresh cilantro, chopped

2 cloves garlic, minced

1/2 cup white wine

Servings: 4

Method: Steam clams with white wine, garlic, and cilantro.

Nutrition: 180 calories; 4g fat; 7g carbs; 25g protein

Braised Octopus with Oregano

Time: 1 hour

Ingredients:

1 whole octopus, cleaned and cut into pieces

2 tablespoons fresh oregano, chopped

2 cups tomatoes, crushed

2 tablespoons olive oil

Servings: 4

Method: Braise octopus with tomatoes and oregano, finish with olive oil.

Nutrition: 230 calories; 7g fat; 8g carbs; 35g protein

Crab and Corn Sauté

Time: 30 minutes

Ingredients:

1 pound crab meat

2 cups corn kernels

2 tablespoons butter

2 tablespoons fresh chives, chopped

Servings: 4

Method: Sauté crab meat and corn in butter, garnish with chives.

Nutrition: 280 calories; 14g fat; 12g carbs; 25g protein

Grilled Eel with Endive

Time: 40 minutes

Ingredients:

2 eel fillets

4 endives, halved

2 tablespoons soy sauce

1 tablespoon sesame oil

Servings: 4

Method: Grill eel, serve with wilted endive and soy-sesame sauce.

Nutrition: 310 calories; 15g fat; 5g carbs; 40g protein

Halibut with Horseradish

Time: 30 minutes

Ingredients:

4 halibut fillets (about 6 oz each)

2 tablespoons horseradish, grated

1 cup beets, roasted and pureed

Juice of 1 lemon

Servings: 4

Method: Sear halibut, serve with horseradish-beet puree, lemon.

Nutrition: 230 calories; 8g fat; 5g carbs; 34g protein

Sardines with Spinach

Time: 20 minutes

Ingredients:

8 fresh sardines

4 cups spinach

2 cloves garlic, minced

2 tomatoes, diced

Servings: 4

Method: Grill sardines, serve on spinach sautéed with garlic and tomatoes.

Nutrition: 210 calories; 10g fat; 4g carbs; 28g protein

Swordfish with Sumac

Time: 25 minutes

Ingredients:

4 swordfish steaks (about 6 oz each)

2 teaspoons sumac

Juice of 2 limes

2 tablespoons olive oil

Servings: 4

Method: Grill swordfish, sprinkle with sumac, lime-infused olive oil.

Nutrition: 250 calories; 9g fat; 1g carbs; 39g protein

Baked Anchovy and Artichoke

Time: 20 minutes

Ingredients:

1 can anchovies

1 can artichoke hearts, drained

2 tablespoons fresh parsley, chopped

2 tablespoons butter, melted

Servings: 4

Method: Bake anchovies on artichoke hearts, finish with parsley butter.

Nutrition: 220 calories; 14g fat; 4g carbs; 22g protein

Roast Trout with Thyme

Time: 25 minutes

Ingredients:

4 trout fillets (about 6 oz each)

2 tablespoons fresh thyme, chopped

1/4 cup almonds, sliced

Zest of 1 lemon

Servings: 4

Method: Roast trout with thyme, garnish with almonds, lemon zest.

Nutrition: 210 calories; 8g fat; 2g carbs; 32g protein

Seared Scallops with Saffron

Time: 20 minutes

Ingredients:

12 large scallops

1 pinch saffron threads

1/2 cup heavy cream

2 tablespoons chives, chopped

Servings: 4

Method: Sear scallops, serve with saffron cream sauce, chives.

Nutrition: 270 calories; 16g fat; 5g carbs; 29g protein

Champagne-Steamed Oysters

Time: 15 minutes

Ingredients:

12 oysters, shucked

1/4 onion, finely chopped

1/2 cup champagne

Freshly ground black pepper

Servings: 2

Method: Steam oysters in champagne with onions, season with pepper.

Nutrition: 110 calories; 3g fat; 7g carbs; 11g protein

Prawn Sauté with Paprika

Time: 20 minutes

Ingredients:

1 pound prawns, peeled and deveined

1 teaspoon paprika

2 cloves garlic, minced

2 tablespoons butter

Servings: 4

Method: Sauté prawns in butter, garlic, paprika.

Nutrition: 180 calories; 8g fat; 1g carbs; 27g protein

Grilled Seabass with Sorrel

Time: 30 minutes

Ingredients:

4 seabass fillets (about 6 oz each)

2 cups sorrel leaves

Zest of 1 orange

2 tablespoons olive oil

Servings: 4

Method: Grill seabass, serve on sorrel, orange-infused olive oil.

Nutrition: 220 calories; 9g fat; 3g carbs; 32g protein

Monkfish with Mango Salsa

Time: 35 minutes

Ingredients:

4 monkfish fillets (about 6 oz each)

1 mango, diced

1 teaspoon chili flakes

1/4 cup coconut, shredded

Servings: 4

Method: Roast monkfish, serve with spicy mango-coconut salsa.

Nutrition: 240 calories; 10g fat; 9g carbs; 32g protein

Vegetarian and Vegan delights

Avocado & Tomato Toast

Time: 10 minutes

Ingredients: 4 slices whole grain bread, 2 ripe avocados, 2 tomatoes, salt, pepper

Servings: 4

Method: Spread mashed avocado on toast, top with tomato slices, season.

Nutrition: Approx. 200 calories per serving; 10g fat; 24g carbs; 6g protein

Quinoa Stuffed Bell Peppers

Time: 45 minutes

Ingredients: 4 bell peppers, 2 cups cooked quinoa, 1 cup black beans, 1 cup corn, 1 tsp cumin

Servings: 4

Method: Stuff mixed quinoa, beans, corn, cumin into bell peppers, bake.

Nutrition: Approx. 220 calories per serving; 3g fat; 40g carbs; 9g protein

Vegan Lentil Soup

Time: 1 hour

Ingredients: 1 cup lentils, 1 onion, 2 carrots, 2 celery stalks, 1 can diced tomatoes, 4 cups vegetable broth

Servings: 4

Method: Sauté vegetables, add lentils, tomatoes, broth, simmer.

Nutrition: Approx. 190 calories per serving; 1g fat; 35g carbs; 11g protein

Tofu Stir-Fry

Time: 30 minutes

Ingredients: 1 block tofu, 2 cups mixed vegetables, 2 tbsp soy sauce, 1 tbsp sesame oil, 1 tsp ginger

Servings: 4

Method: Stir-fry tofu, add vegetables and ginger, stir in sauces.

Nutrition: Approx. 180 calories per serving; 9g fat; 12g carbs; 16g protein

Spinach & Mushroom Frittata

Time: 40 minutes

Ingredients: 1 cup spinach, 1 cup mushrooms, 4 eggs, 1/4 cup milk, 1/4 cup cheese (optional)

Servings: 4

Method: Sauté spinach and mushrooms, add beaten eggs and milk, bake until set.

Nutrition: Approx. 150 calories per serving; 9g fat; 5g carbs; 12g protein

Veggie Sushi Rolls

Time: 30 minutes

Ingredients: 2 cups sushi rice, 4 nori sheets, 1 cucumber, 1 avocado, 1 bell pepper

Servings: 4

Method: Spread rice on nori, add sliced veggies, roll, slice.

Nutrition: Approx. 240 calories per roll; 4g fat; 46g carbs; 6g protein

Cauliflower Buffalo Wings

Time: 40 minutes

Ingredients: 1 head cauliflower, 1 cup buffalo sauce, 1 cup flour, 1 cup water

Servings: 4

Method: Dip cauliflower in batter, bake, toss in buffalo sauce.

Nutrition: Approx. 210 calories per serving; 6g fat; 34g carbs; 6g protein

Chickpea Salad Sandwich

Time: 15 minutes

Ingredients: 1 can chickpeas, 1/4 cup vegan mayo, 1 celery stalk, 2 tbsp onion, 4 bread slices

Servings: 4

Method: Mash chickpeas, mix with mayo, celery, onion, spread on bread.

Nutrition: Approx. 350 calories per sandwich; 12g fat; 50g carbs; 12g protein

Sweet Potato & Black Bean Burritos

Time: 50 minutes

Ingredients: 2 sweet potatoes, 1 can black beans, 4 tortillas, 1 cup salsa, 1 avocado

Servings: 4

Method: Roast sweet potatoes, mix with beans, wrap in tortillas with salsa, avocado.

Nutrition: Approx. 380 calories per burrito; 9g fat; 65g carbs; 12g protein

Vegan Pad Thai

Time: 30 minutes

Ingredients: 8 oz rice noodles, 1 cup tofu, 2 cups mixed veggies, 1/4 cup peanut sauce

Servings: 4

Method: Cook noodles, stir-fry tofu and veggies, mix with noodles and sauce.

Nutrition: Approx. 320 calories per serving; 10g fat; 48g carbs; 14g protein

Veggie Burger with Sweet Potato Fries

Time: 45 minutes

Ingredients: 4 veggie patties, 4 whole grain buns, 2 sweet potatoes, 1 tbsp olive oil

Servings: 4

Method: Bake sweet potato fries, grill burgers, serve on buns.

Nutrition: Approx. 420 calories per serving; 14g fat; 60g carbs; 20g protein

Vegan Pizza with Veggie Toppings

Time: 30 minutes (excluding dough prep)

Ingredients: 1 pizza dough, 1/2 cup tomato sauce, 1 cup vegan cheese, 2 cups assorted veggies

Servings: 4

Method: Spread sauce on dough, top with cheese and veggies, bake.

Nutrition: Approx. 280 calories per slice; 9g fat; 40g carbs; 10g protein

Zucchini Noodles with Tomato Sauce

Time: 20 minutes

Ingredients: 4 zucchinis, 2 cups tomato sauce, 1 tbsp olive oil, 1 tsp garlic

Servings: 4

Method: Spiralize zucchinis, sauté with garlic, mix with tomato sauce.

Nutrition: Approx. 120 calories per serving; 7g fat; 14g carbs; 4g protein

Vegan Mac and Cheese

Time: 35 minutes

Ingredients: 2 cups macaroni, 1 cup cashews, 1/4 cup nutritional yeast, 1 cup almond milk

Servings: 4

Method: Cook macaroni, blend cashews, yeast, milk for sauce, mix together.

Nutrition: Approx. 350 calories per serving; 15g fat; 45g carbs; 12g protein

Stuffed Mushrooms with Spinach & Quinoa

Time: 40 minutes

Ingredients: 12 large mushrooms, 1 cup cooked quinoa, 1 cup spinach, 1/4 cup breadcrumbs

Servings: 4

Method: Stuff mushrooms with quinoa, spinach, top with breadcrumbs, bake.

Nutrition: Approx. 150 calories per serving; 3g fat; 24g carbs; 8g protein

Roasted Vegetable Salad

Time: 40 minutes

Ingredients: 4 cups mixed vegetables (carrots, bell peppers, onions), 1/4 cup olive oil, 2 tbsp balsamic vinegar

Servings: 4

Method: Roast vegetables, mix with olive oil and vinegar.

Nutrition: Approx. 200 calories per serving; 14g fat; 20g carbs; 4g protein

Vegan Chili

Time: 1 hour

Ingredients: 1 cup kidney beans, 1 cup black beans, 2 cups diced tomatoes, 1 onion, 1 bell pepper, 1 tsp cumin

Servings: 4

Method: Cook all ingredients until flavors meld.

Nutrition: Approx. 240 calories per serving; 1g fat; 45g carbs; 13g protein

Grilled Vegetable Skewers

Time: 25 minutes

Ingredients: 2 bell peppers, 2 zucchinis, 1 onion, 1/4 cup olive oil, 1 tsp herbs

Servings: 4

Method: Skewer chopped vegetables, brush with oil and herbs, grill.

Nutrition: Approx. 150 calories per serving; 14g fat; 10g carbs; 2g protein

Vegan Shepherd's Pie

Time: 1 hour

Ingredients: 2 cups lentils, 1 cup peas, 1 cup carrots, 2 cups mashed potatoes

Servings: 6

Method: Layer lentils, vegetables, and mashed potatoes in a dish, bake.

Nutrition: Approx. 320 calories per serving; 6g fat; 54g carbs; 14g prote

Soups

Tempeh with Turmeric

Time: 30 minutes

Ingredients:

1 block tempeh (about 8 oz)

1 teaspoon turmeric

2 cups broccoli, cut into florets

1/4 cup almonds, sliced and toasted

Servings: 4

Method: Sauté tempeh with turmeric, serve with steamed broccoli, top with roasted almonds.

Nutrition: 220 calories; 12g fat; 16g carbs; 20g protein

Quinoa with Quince

Time: 25 minutes

Ingredients:

2 cups cooked quinoa

1 medium quince, roasted and diced

2 cups fresh spinach, chopped

1/4 cup pecans, crushed

Servings: 4

Method: Mix cooked quinoa with roasted quince, spinach, and crushed pecans.

Nutrition: 190 calories; 6g fat; 30g carbs; 8g protein

Portobello Mushrooms with Parsnip

Time: 35 minutes

Ingredients:

4 large portobello mushrooms

2 medium parsnips, peeled and sliced

2 cloves garlic, minced

1 teaspoon fresh thyme, chopped

68

Servings: 4

Method: Grill portobellos, serve over roasted parsnips with garlic and thyme.

Nutrition: 140 calories; 3g fat; 27g carbs; 5g protein

Lentil and Leek Stew

Time: 40 minutes

Ingredients:

1 cup green lentils, rinsed

2 leeks, cleaned and chopped

2 carrots, diced

1 can coconut milk (13.5 oz)

Servings: 6

Method: Simmer lentils with leeks and carrots in coconut broth.

Nutrition: 180 calories; 7g fat; 24g carbs; 9g protein

Seitan with Sage

Time: 30 minutes

Ingredients:

1 lb seitan, sliced

2 tablespoons fresh sage, chopped

4 medium potatoes, boiled and mashed

1/4 cup walnuts, chopped

Servings: 4

Method: Sauté seitan with sage, serve over mashed potatoes, top with walnuts.

Nutrition: 210 calories; 8g fat; 28g carbs; 22g protein

Chickpea and Chard Stir-Fry

Time: 30 minutes

Ingredients:

2 cups chickpeas, cooked

4 cups Swiss chard, chopped

1 cup tomatoes, diced

Zest of 1 lemon

Servings: 4

Method: Stir-fry chickpeas and chard, add tomatoes, finish with lemon zest.

Nutrition: 180 calories; 4g fat; 32g carbs; 8g protein

Tofu with Tarragon

Time: 25 minutes

Ingredients:

1 block tofu (14 oz), pressed and cubed

2 tablespoons fresh tarragon, chopped

2 bell peppers, sliced

2 tablespoons sesame seeds

Servings: 4

Method: Pan-sear tofu with tarragon, serve with sautéed bell peppers, sprinkle with sesame.

Nutrition: 210 calories; 12g fat; 9g carbs; 20g protein

Butternut Squash with Basil

Time: 40 minutes

Ingredients:

1 medium butternut squash, cubed

1/4 cup fresh basil, chopped

1 onion, diced

1/4 cup hazelnuts, chopped

Servings: 4

Method: Roast butternut, mix with caramelized onion and basil, top with hazelnuts.

Nutrition: 190 calories; 8g fat; 29g carbs; 4g protein

Cauliflower with Cumin

Time: 30 minutes

Ingredients:

1 head cauliflower, cut into florets

1 teaspoon cumin

1/4 cup almonds, sliced

2 tablespoons parsley, chopped

Servings: 4

Method: Roast cauliflower with cumin, top with almonds, parsley.

Nutrition: 160 calories; 10g fat; 15g carbs; 7g protein

Eggplant with Endive

Time: 35 minutes

Ingredients:

2 large eggplants, sliced

2 heads endive, sliced

2 tablespoons olive oil

1 tablespoon fresh tarragon, chopped

Servings: 4

Method: Grill eggplant, top with sautéed endive, drizzle olive oil, sprinkle tarragon.

Nutrition: 170 calories; 12g fat; 15g carbs; 3g protein

Spinach Salad with Sunflower Seeds

Time: 20 minutes

Ingredients:

8 cups fresh spinach

1/4 cup sunflower seeds

2 avocados, sliced

Dill dressing (to taste)

Servings: 4

Method: Toss spinach with avocado, sunflower seeds, dill dressing.

Nutrition: 150 calories; 11g fat; 9g carbs; 5g protein

Radish Salad with Rosemary

Time: 15 minutes

Ingredients:

2 cups radishes, thinly sliced

1 tablespoon fresh rosemary, chopped

Lemon-tahini dressing (to taste)

Servings: 4

Method: Mix sliced radishes with rosemary, lemon-tahini dressing.

Nutrition: 80 calories; 3g fat; 11g carbs; 2g protein

Beet and Buckwheat Salad

Time: 40 minutes

Ingredients:

4 medium beets, roasted and cubed

2 cups cooked buckwheat

1 fennel bulb, thinly sliced

1/4 cup walnuts, chopped

Servings: 4

Method: Roast beets, serve on buckwheat with fennel, top with walnuts.

Nutrition: 190 calories; 6g fat; 32g carbs; 7g protein

Grilled Zucchini with Za'atar

Time: 25 minutes

Ingredients:

4 zucchinis, sliced lengthwise

2 teaspoons za'atar spice mix

1 cup cooked chickpeas

1 tablespoon sesame oil

Servings: 4

Method: Grill zucchini with za'atar, toss with chickpeas, sesame oil.

Nutrition: 170 calories; 8g fat; 20g carbs; 6g protein

Sweet Potato Wedges with Sage

Time: 45 minutes

Ingredients:

3 large sweet potatoes, cut into wedges

2 tablespoons fresh sage, chopped

2 tablespoons maple syrup

1/4 cup cashews, chopped

Servings: 4

Method: Grill sweet potatoes, drizzle with maple syrup, sage, top with cashews.

Nutrition: 210 calories; 7g fat; 37g carbs; 4g protein

Kale Salad with Kelp Noodles

Time: 20 minutes

Ingredients:

4 cups kale, chopped

2 cups kelp noodles

2 tablespoons garlic-infused olive oil

1/4 cup almonds, slivered

Servings: 4

Method: Massage kale with garlic oil, toss with kelp noodles, top with almonds.

Nutrition: 120 calories; 8g fat; 10g carbs; 4g protein

Parsley and Pumpkin Seed Salad

Time: 15 minutes

Ingredients:

2 cups parsley, chopped

1/4 cup pumpkin seeds, toasted

Lime-tahini dressing (to taste)

Servings: 4

Method: Chop parsley, mix with pumpkin seeds, lime-tahini dressing.

Nutrition: 90 calories; 6g fat; 6g carbs; 4g protein

Tomato and Tofu Sauté

Time: 30 minutes

Ingredients:

14 oz firm tofu, drained and cubed

2 large tomatoes, diced

1/4 cup fresh basil, chopped

2 tablespoons hemp seeds

Servings: 4

Method: Sauté tofu with tomatoes and basil, finish with hemp seeds.

Nutrition: 160 calories; 8g fat; 10g carbs; 14g protein

Cabbage Salad with Cilantro

Time: 20 minutes

Ingredients:

4 cups cabbage, shredded

1 large apple, diced

1/4 cup fresh cilantro, chopped

1/4 cup dill vinaigrette

Servings: 4

Method: Toss cabbage with apple, cilantro, dill vinaigrette.

Nutrition: 80 calories; 1g fat; 20g carbs; 2g protein

Quinoa with Quince

Time: 35 minutes

Ingredients:

2 cups cooked quinoa

1 large quince, roasted and diced

Zest of 1 lemon

1/4 cup pine nuts, toasted

Servings: 4

Method: Cook quinoa, mix with quince, lemon zest, toasted pine nuts.

Nutrition: 210 calories; 8g fat; 32g carbs; 6g protein

Quick Bites

Pesto Spread

Time: 15 minutes

Ingredients:

2 cups fresh basil leaves

1/3 cup pine nuts

2 cloves garlic

1/2 cup grated Parmesan cheese

Olive oil as needed for consistency

Servings: 8 bites

Method: Blend basil, pine nuts, garlic, and Parmesan into pesto, serve on crackers.

Nutrition: 95 calories; 7g fat; 3g carbs; 4g protein

Guacamole

Time: 10 minutes

Ingredients:

3 ripe avocados

1 medium tomato, diced

1/4 cup diced red onion

Juice of 1 lime

Salt to taste

Servings: 8 servings

Method: Mash avocado, mix with diced tomatoes, onions, and lime juice.

Nutrition: 110 calories; 9g fat; 7g carbs; 2g protein

Hummus Dip

Time: 15 minutes

Ingredients:

1 can (15 oz) chickpeas, drained and rinsed

1/4 cup tahini

Juice of 1 lemon

1-2 cloves garlic

Salt to taste

Servings: 8 servings

Method: Blend chickpeas, tahini, lemon, and garlic into a smooth hummus, serve with veggies.

Nutrition: 105 calories; 5g fat; 12g carbs; 5g protein

Mango Chili Mix

Time: 10 minutes

Ingredients:

2 large mangos, peeled and cubed

1 teaspoon chili powder, adjust to taste

Juice of 1 lime

Pinch of sea salt

Servings: 8 bites

Method: Toss mango chunks with chili, lime juice, and sea salt.

Nutrition: 45 calories; 0.2g fat; 11g carbs; 1g protein

Tomato Bruschetta

Time: 12 minutes

Ingredients:

3 medium tomatoes, diced

1/4 cup fresh basil, chopped

2 cloves garlic, minced

2 tablespoons olive oil

8 slices of baguette, toasted

Servings: 8 bites

Method: Mix diced tomatoes, garlic, basil, olive oil, serve on toast.

Nutrition: 70 calories; 3g fat; 9g carbs; 2g protein

Olive and Feta Mix

Time: 10 minutes

Ingredients:

1 cup mixed olives

1/2 cup feta cheese, crumbled

1 tablespoon fresh rosemary, chopped

Juice of 1/2 lemon

Servings: 8 bites

Method: Combine olives, crumbled feta, rosemary, and lemon juice.

Nutrition: 90 calories; 8g fat; 3g carbs; 3g protein

Caprese Salad

Time: 12 minutes

Ingredients:

4 medium tomatoes, sliced

8 oz fresh mozzarella cheese, sliced

1/4 cup fresh basil leaves

Balsamic reduction for drizzling

Servings: 8 bites

Method: Layer tomato, mozzarella, basil, drizzle with balsamic.

Nutrition: 85 calories; 5g fat; 5g carbs; 5g protein

Tzatziki Sauce

Time: 15 minutes

Ingredients:

1 medium cucumber, grated and drained

1 cup Greek yogurt

2 tablespoons fresh dill, chopped

1 clove garlic, minced

Servings: 8 servings

Method: Mix grated cucumber, yogurt, dill, and garlic.

Nutrition: 40 calories; 1g fat; 5g carbs; 3g protein

Creamy Spinach Dip

Time: 14 minutes

Ingredients:

2 cups fresh spinach, chopped

1/2 cup cream cheese

1/4 teaspoon nutmeg

1 clove garlic, minced

Servings: 8 bites

Method: Sauté spinach and garlic, mix with cream cheese, add nutmeg.

Nutrition: 70 calories; 5g fat; 3g carbs; 3g protein

Feta and Watermelon Salad

Time: 13 minutes

Ingredients:

2 cups watermelon, cubed

1/2 cup feta cheese, cubed

2 tablespoons fresh mint, chopped

Black pepper to taste

Servings: 8 bites

Method: Cube watermelon, feta, toss with mint, black pepper.

Nutrition: 60 calories; 3g fat; 8g carbs; 2g protein

Quinoa Salad

Time: 15 minutes

Ingredients:

2 cups cooked quinoa

1 cup cherry tomatoes, halved

1 cup cucumber, diced

Juice of 1 lemon

Servings: 8 bites

Method: Mix quinoa, cherry tomatoes, cucumber, drizzle lemon juice.

Nutrition: 120 calories; 2g fat; 22g carbs; 4g protein

Garlic Roasted Edamame

Time: 10 minutes

Ingredients:

2 cups edamame, shelled

1 teaspoon sea salt

2 cloves garlic, minced

Servings: 8 servings

Method: Toss edamame with garlic, sea salt, roast until golden.

Nutrition: 100 calories; 4g fat; 8g carbs; 9g protein

Ricotta and Honey Cracker

Time: 12 minutes

Ingredients:

1 cup ricotta cheese

2 tablespoons honey

1/4 cup almond slivers

8 whole-grain crackers

Servings: 8 bites

Method: Spread ricotta on crackers, drizzle with honey, top with almonds.

Nutrition: 85 calories; 5g fat; 7g carbs; 4g protein

Spicy Avocado Toast

Time: 10 minutes

Ingredients:

2 ripe avocados

1 teaspoon chili flakes

Juice of 1 lemon

8 slices of whole-grain bread, toasted

Servings: 8 bites

Method: Mash avocado, mix with chili flakes, lemon, spread on toast.

Nutrition: 120 calories; 10g fat; 8g carbs; 2g protein

Beet and Goat Cheese Bites

Time: 15 minutes

Ingredients:

2 medium beets, roasted and sliced

4 oz goat cheese

1/4 cup walnuts, crushed

Servings: 8 bites

Method: Layer roasted beets with goat cheese, top with walnuts.

Nutrition: 90 calories; 6g fat; 6g carbs; 4g protein

Smoked Salmon on Rye

Time: 12 minutes

Ingredients:

8 slices rye bread

8 oz smoked salmon

4 oz cream cheese

Servings: 8 bites

Method: Spread cream cheese on rye, top with smoked salmon.

Nutrition: 110 calories; 5g fat; 9g carbs; 7g protein

Cucumber Yogurt Bites

Time: 10 minutes

Ingredients:

2 large cucumbers, sliced

1 cup Greek yogurt

2 tablespoons fresh dill, chopped

Servings: 8 bites

Method: Mix yogurt and dill, spread on cucumber slices.

Nutrition: 35 calories; 1g fat; 4g carbs; 2g protein

Blueberry Yogurt Parfait

Time: 10 minutes

Ingredients:

2 cups fresh blueberries

2 cups Greek yogurt

2 tablespoons honey

Servings: 8 servings

Method: Layer blueberries and yogurt, drizzle with honey.

Nutrition: 95 calories; 1g fat; 17g carbs; 5g protein

Baked Fig with Brie

Time: 12 minutes

Ingredients:

8 fresh figs, halved

4 oz Brie cheese

1/4 cup walnuts, chopped

Servings: 8 bites

Method: Top fig halves with Brie and walnut, bake until melted.

Nutrition: 80 calories; 5g fat; 7g carbs; 3g protein

Mango Chili Cubes

Time: 10 minutes

Ingredients:

2 large mangos, peeled and cubed

1 teaspoon chili powder

Juice of 1 lime

Servings: 8 bites

Method: Cube mango, sprinkle with chili powder, lime.

Nutrition: 60 calories; 0.5g fat; 15g carbs; 1g protein

Dessert Heaven

Chocolate Avocado Mousse

Time: 20 minutes

Ingredients:

4 oz dark chocolate

2 ripe avocados

3 tablespoons honey

Servings: 8

Method: Melt chocolate, blend with avocado and honey to create a mousse.

Nutrition: 150 calories; 9g fat; 18g carbs; 2g protein

Berry Yogurt Parfait

Time: 15 minutes

Ingredients:

2 cups mixed berries

2 cups Greek yogurt

1/4 cup almonds, crushed

Servings: 6

Method: Layer berries with yogurt and crushed almonds.

Nutrition: 110 calories; 3g fat; 15g carbs; 5g protein

Grilled Honey Cinnamon Pears

Time: 25 minutes

Ingredients:

3 large pears

1 teaspoon cinnamon

3 tablespoons honey

Servings: 6

Method: Slice pears, drizzle with honey and cinnamon, grill until caramelized.

Nutrition: 95 calories; 0.5g fat; 25g carbs; 1g protein

Ricotta-Stuffed Figs with Pistachios

Time: 20 minutes

Ingredients:

12 fresh figs

1 cup ricotta cheese

1/4 cup pistachios, chopped

Servings: 6

Method: Stuff figs with ricotta, sprinkle with pistachios.

Nutrition: 110 calories; 5g fat; 14g carbs; 3g protein

Banana Coconut Layered Dessert

Time: 20 minutes

Ingredients:

4 ripe bananas, sliced

2 cups coconut cream

1 teaspoon vanilla extract

Servings: 8

Method: Layer banana slices with coconut cream and vanilla.

Nutrition: 140 calories; 8g fat; 17g carbs; 2g protein

Baked Apple Oatmeal

Time: 30 minutes

Ingredients:

3 medium apples, diced

2 cups oats

1/4 cup maple syrup

Servings: 6

Method: Combine diced apples with oats and maple syrup, bake.

Nutrition: 125 calories; 2g fat; 27g carbs; 3g protein

Grilled Peaches with Almonds

Time: 25 minutes

Ingredients:

6 peaches, halved

1/4 cup almonds, slivered

1 teaspoon cinnamon

Servings: 6

Method: Grill sliced peaches with cinnamon, top with almonds.

Nutrition: 85 calories; 2g fat; 17g carbs; 2g protein

Raspberry Chocolate Mint Dessert

Time: 15 minutes

Ingredients:

2 cups raspberries

4 oz dark chocolate, melted

Fresh mint leaves for garnish

Servings: 8

Method: Drizzle raspberries with melted chocolate, garnish with mint.

Nutrition: 100 calories; 4g fat; 14g carbs; 2g protein

Roasted Pineapple with Chili

Time: 20 minutes

Ingredients:

1 pineapple, sliced

1 teaspoon chili powder

Juice of 1 lime

Servings: 6

Method: Roast pineapple slices with chili, finish with lime.

Nutrition: 70 calories; 0g fat; 18g carbs; 1g protein

Stuffed Dates with Walnuts

Time: 15 minutes

Ingredients:

16 dates, pitted

16 walnut halves

2 tablespoons honey

Servings: 8

Method: Stuff dates with walnuts, drizzle with honey.

Nutrition: 110 calories; 4g fat; 20g carbs; 2g protein

Mango Chia Pudding

Time: 15 minutes

Ingredients:

2 ripe mangos, pureed

1/2 cup chia seeds

2 cups almond milk

Servings: 6

Method: Puree mango, layer with chia seeds in almond milk.

Nutrition: 140 calories; 4g fat; 25g carbs; 3g protein

Blueberry Yogurt Blend

Time: 20 minutes

Ingredients:

2 cups blueberries

2 cups Greek yogurt

2 tablespoons honey

Servings: 8

Method: Blend blueberries with yogurt and honey.

Nutrition: 130 calories; 2g fat; 25g carbs; 5g protein

Lemon Almond Maple Treat

Time: 25 minutes

Ingredients:

Zest of 2 lemons

2 cups almond flour

1/4 cup maple syrup

Servings: 8

Method: Create almond flour base with lemon zest, drizzle maple syrup.

Nutrition: 150 calories; 8g fat; 16g carbs; 4g protein

Chocolate Cherry Delight

Time: 20 minutes

Ingredients:

2 cups cherries, pitted

4 oz dark chocolate, melted

1 teaspoon vanilla extract

Servings: 6

Method: Mix melted chocolate with cherries and vanilla.

Nutrition: 160 calories; 7g fat; 24g carbs; 2g protein

Kiwi Coconut Honey Layers

Time: 15 minutes

Ingredients:

4 ripe kiwis, sliced

2 cups whipped coconut cream

3 tablespoons honey

Servings: 6

Method: Layer kiwi with whipped coconut cream, honey.

Nutrition: 140 calories; 8g fat; 18g carbs; 2g protein

Strawberry Oat Almond Bake

Time: 25 minutes

Ingredients:

2 cups strawberries, diced

2 cups oats

1/2 cup almond butter

Servings: 8

Method: Bake diced strawberries with oats and almond butter.

Nutrition: 165 calories; 9g fat; 20g carbs; 4g protein

Pomegranate Chocolate Pistachio Bite

Time: 15 minutes

Ingredients:

1 cup pomegranate seeds

4 oz dark chocolate, melted

1/4 cup pistachios, crushed

Servings: 6

Method: Drizzle pomegranate seeds with chocolate, top with pistachios.

Nutrition: 155 calories; 7g fat; 22g carbs; 3g protein

Stuffed Apricots with Ricotta

Time: 20 minutes

Ingredients:

12 apricots, halved

1 cup ricotta cheese

1/4 cup walnuts, crushed

Servings: 6

Method: Stuff apricots with ricotta, top with walnuts.

Nutrition: 130 calories; 6g fat; 18g carbs; 4g protein

Cranberry Yogurt Mix

Time: 20 minutes

Ingredients:

1 cup cranberries, fresh or frozen

2 cups Greek yogurt

2 tablespoons honey

Servings: 8

Method: Combine cranberries with yogurt and honey.

Nutrition: 135 calories; 2g fat; 25g carbs; 5g protein

Passionfruit Coconut Chia Layer

Time: 15 minutes

Ingredients:

6 passionfruits, pulp scooped out

2 cups coconut milk

1/2 cup chia seeds

Servings: 6

Method: Layer passionfruit with chia seeds in coconut milk.

Nutrition: 145 calories; 8g fat; 18g carbs; 3g protein

Gluten free recipes

Quinoa Vegetable Salad

Time: 25 minutes

Ingredients:

1 cup quinoa, uncooked

2 cups mixed vegetables (bell peppers, cucumbers, tomatoes), chopped

Juice of 1 lemon

Servings: 6

Method: Cook quinoa, mix with chopped vegetables, dress with lemon juice.

Nutrition: 180 calories; 3g fat; 32g carbs; 6g protein

Almond Flour Blueberry Muffins

Time: 20 minutes

Ingredients:

2 cups almond flour

3 large eggs

1 cup blueberries

Servings: 10 muffins

Method: Combine almond flour with eggs, fold in blueberries, bake.

Nutrition: 150 calories; 9g fat; 14g carbs; 5g protein

Grilled Parmesan Zucchini

Time: 30 minutes

Ingredients:

4 medium zucchinis, sliced lengthwise

1/2 cup grated Parmesan cheese

2 tablespoons olive oil

Servings: 4

Method: Slice zucchini, sprinkle with Parmesan, grill until golden.

Nutrition: 120 calories; 8g fat; 7g carbs; 6g protein

Chia Coconut Mango Pudding

Time: 10 minutes plus chilling

Ingredients:

1/4 cup chia seeds

2 cups coconut milk

1 ripe mango, pureed

Servings: 4

Method: Mix chia seeds with coconut milk, layer with mango puree.

Nutrition: 190 calories; 10g fat; 24g carbs; 5g protein

Creamy Cauliflower Mash

Time: 40 minutes

Ingredients:

1 large head cauliflower, cut into florets

2 cloves garlic, minced

2 tablespoons olive oil

Servings: 4

Method: Blend roasted cauliflower with garlic and olive oil into a mash.

Nutrition: 110 calories; 7g fat; 10g carbs; 3g protein

Coconut Banana Cocoa Cookies

Time: 20 minutes

Ingredients:

1 cup coconut flour

2 ripe bananas, mashed

2 tablespoons cocoa powder

Servings: 12 cookies

Method: Mix ingredients, form cookies, bake until golden.

Nutrition: 140 calories; 6g fat; 18g carbs; 3g protein

Buckwheat Berry Breakfast

Time: 30 minutes

Ingredients:

1 cup buckwheat groats

3 cups almond milk

2 cups mixed berries

Servings: 4

Method: Cook buckwheat in almond milk, top with fresh berries.

Nutrition: 175 calories; 3g fat; 35g carbs; 5g protein

Chickpea Flour Spinach Pancakes

Time: 40 minutes

Ingredients:

1 cup chickpea flour

2 cups fresh spinach, chopped

3 tablespoons olive oil

Servings: 4

Method: Mix chickpea flour with water and spinach, cook as pancakes.

Nutrition: 160 calories; 6g fat; 20g carbs; 7g protein

Rosemary Parmesan Polenta

Time: 25 minutes

Ingredients:

1 cup cornmeal

1 tablespoon fresh rosemary, chopped

1/4 cup grated Parmesan cheese

Servings: 4

Method: Cook cornmeal, infuse with rosemary, top with Parmesan.

Nutrition: 190 calories; 4g fat; 32g carbs; 6g protein

Brown Rice Veggie Blend

Time: 45 minutes

Ingredients:

1 cup brown rice, uncooked

1 bell pepper, chopped

1 onion, chopped

Servings: 6

Method: Cook rice, sauté with bell peppers and onions.

Nutrition: 210 calories; 2g fat; 44g carbs; 5g protein

Sunflower Seed Date Bars

Time: 15 minutes

Ingredients:

1 cup sunflower seeds

1 cup dates, pitted

2 tablespoons cocoa powder

Servings: 8 bars

Method: Blend sunflower seeds, dates, and cocoa; press into bars; chill.

Nutrition: 180 calories; 9g fat; 21g carbs; 6g protein

Millet Kale Bowl

Time: 35 minutes

Ingredients:

1 cup millet, uncooked

2 cups kale, chopped

1/4 cup pumpkin seeds

Servings: 4

Method: Cook millet, toss with sautéed kale, top with pumpkin seeds.

Nutrition: 210 calories; 7g fat; 30g carbs; 8g protein

Vanilla Tapioca Pudding

Time: 20 minutes

Ingredients:

1/2 cup tapioca pearls

2 cups almond milk

1 teaspoon vanilla extract

Servings: 4

Method: Cook tapioca in almond milk, flavor with vanilla.

Nutrition: 150 calories; 3g fat; 28g carbs; 1g protein

Sorghum Mushroom Medley

Time: 40 minutes

Ingredients:

1 cup sorghum, uncooked

2 cups mushrooms, sliced

1 tablespoon fresh thyme, chopped

Servings: 4

Method: Cook sorghum, mix with sautéed mushrooms and thyme.

Nutrition: 220 calories; 4g fat; 42g carbs; 7g protein

Macadamia Chocolate Clusters

Time: 15 minutes

Ingredients:

1 cup macadamia nuts

4 ounces dark chocolate, melted

Pinch of sea salt

Servings: 8 clusters

Method: Melt chocolate, mix with macadamias, form clusters, chill.

Nutrition: 190 calories; 14g fat; 12g carbs; 2g protein

Amaranth Black Bean Bowl

Time: 30 minutes

Ingredients:

1 cup amaranth, uncooked

1 can black beans, drained and rinsed

1/4 cup fresh cilantro, chopped

Servings: 4

Method: Cook amaranth, mix with black beans, garnish with cilantro.

Nutrition: 220 calories; 2g fat; 40g carbs; 9g protein

Homemade Hazelnut Cocoa Spread

Time: 20 minutes

Ingredients:

1 cup hazelnuts

2 tablespoons cocoa powder

2 tablespoons honey

Servings: 1 jar

Method: Blend hazelnuts with cocoa and honey into a spread.

Nutrition: 190 calories; 15g fat; 12g carbs; 4g protein

Apple Cinnamon Teff Porridge

Time: 40 minutes

Ingredients:

1 cup teff grain, uncooked

2 apples, diced

1 teaspoon ground cinnamon

Servings: 4

Method: Cook teff, add sautéed apples, sprinkle cinnamon.

Nutrition: 205 calories; 2g fat; 42g carbs; 7g protein

Maple Glazed Pecans

Time: 15 minutes

Ingredients:

1 cup pecans

2 tablespoons maple syrup

Pinch of sea salt

Servings: 8 clusters

Method: Toss pecans with maple syrup, bake, finish with sea salt.

Nutrition: 210 calories; 20g fat; 9g carbs; 3g protein

Blueberry Flaxseed Yogurt Bowl

Time: 20 minutes

Ingredients:

1/4 cup flax seeds

1 cup blueberries

2 cups yogurt

Servings: 4 bowls

Method: Mix flax seeds with blueberries, layer over yogurt.

Nutrition: 180 calories; 7g fat; 22g carbs; 5g protein

30 Days meal plain

Week 1

Day 1

Breakfast: Chia's Cosmic Concerto

Lunch: Quinoa's Quiet Quest

Dinner: Zucchini's Zenful Zephyr

Day 2

Breakfast: Almond's Ambient Aria (Muffins)

Lunch: Polenta's Planetary Praise

Dinner: Rice's Radiant Rhapsody

Day 3

Breakfast: Blueberry's Blissful Ballad (Yogurt)

Lunch: Chickpea's Cosmic Choir (Savory Pancakes)

Dinner: Cauliflower's Celestial Carol

Day 4

Breakfast: Tapioca's Tranquil Tune

Lunch: Millet's Melodious Murmur

Dinner: Sorghum's Soulful Serenade

Day 5

Breakfast: Amaranth's Aerial Anthem

Lunch: Coconut's Celestial Crescendo (Cookies)

Dinner: Buckwheat's Blissful Ballad

Day 6

Breakfast: Sunflower's Serene Sonata (Bars)

Lunch: Macadamia's Majestic Muse (Clusters)

Dinner: Teff's Timeless Tune

Day 7

Breakfast: Chocolate's Charming Chant (Mousse)

Lunch: Berry's Blissful Ballet (Parfait)

Dinner: Fig's Fantasy Flight

Week 2

Day 8

Breakfast: Lemon's Lyrical Lullaby

Lunch: Quinoa's Quiet Quest

Dinner: Zucchini's Zenful Zephyr

Day 9

Breakfast: Almond's Ambient Aria (Muffins)

Lunch: Chickpea's Cosmic Choir (Savory Pancakes)

Dinner: Rice's Radiant Rhapsody

Day 10

Breakfast: Blueberry's Blissful Ballad (Yogurt)

Lunch: Polenta's Planetary Praise

Dinner: Cauliflower's Celestial Carol

Day 11

Breakfast: Tapioca's Tranquil Tune

Lunch: Millet's Melodious Murmur

Dinner: Sorghum's Soulful Serenade

Day 12

Breakfast: Amaranth's Aerial Anthem

Lunch: Coconut's Celestial Crescendo (Cookies)

Dinner: Buckwheat's Blissful Ballad

Day 13

Breakfast: Sunflower's Serene Sonata (Bars)

Lunch: Macadamia's Majestic Muse (Clusters)

Dinner: Teff's Timeless Tune

Day 14

Breakfast: Chocolate's Charming Chant (Mousse)

Lunch: Berry's Blissful Ballet (Parfait)

Dinner: Fig's Fantasy Flight

Week 3

Day 15

Breakfast: Lemon's Lyrical Lullaby

Lunch: Chickpea's Cosmic Choir (Savory Pancakes)

Dinner: Zucchini's Zenful Zephyr

Day 16

Breakfast: Almond's Ambient Aria (Muffins)

Lunch: Rice's Radiant Rhapsody

Dinner: Polenta's Planetary Praise

Day 17

Breakfast: Blueberry's Blissful Ballad (Yogurt)

Lunch: Quinoa's Quiet Quest

Dinner: Cauliflower's Celestial Carol

Day 18

Breakfast: Tapioca's Tranquil Tune

Lunch: Millet's Melodious Murmur

Dinner: Sorghum's Soulful Serenade

Day 19

Breakfast: Amaranth's Aerial Anthem

Lunch: Coconut's Celestial Crescendo (Cookies)

Dinner: Buckwheat's Blissful Ballad

Day 20

Breakfast: Sunflower's Serene Sonata (Bars)

Lunch: Macadamia's Majestic Muse (Clusters)

Dinner: Teff's Timeless Tune

Day 21

Breakfast: Chocolate's Charming Chant (Mousse)

Lunch: Berry's Blissful Ballet (Parfait)

Dinner: Fig's Fantasy Flight

Week 4

Day 22

Breakfast: Lemon's Lyrical Lullaby

Lunch: Rice's Radiant Rhapsody

Dinner: Zucchini's Zenful Zephyr

Day 23

Breakfast: Almond's Ambient Aria (Muffins)

Lunch: Polenta's Planetary Praise

Dinner: Chickpea's Cosmic Choir (Savory Pancakes)

Day 24

Breakfast: Blueberry's Blissful Ballad (Yogurt)

Lunch: Quinoa's Quiet Quest

Dinner: Cauliflower's Celestial Carol

Day 25

Breakfast: Tapioca's Tranquil Tune

Lunch: Millet's Melodious Murmur

Dinner: Sorghum's Soulful Serenade

Day 26

Breakfast: Amaranth's Aerial Anthem

Lunch: Coconut's Celestial Crescendo (Cookies)

Dinner: Buckwheat's Blissful Ballad

Day 27

Breakfast: Sunflower's Serene Sonata (Bars)

Lunch: Macadamia's Majestic Muse (Clusters)

Dinner: Teff's Timeless Tune

Day 28

Breakfast: Chocolate's Charming Chant (Mousse)

Lunch: Berry's Blissful Ballet (Parfait)

Dinner: Fig's Fantasy Flight

Chapter 4 "Beyond the Plate"

Delve into heart-healthy habits beyond just di

In an urban city on the East Coast, where skyscrapers cast long shadows and the constant hustle and bustle is akin to a relentless heartbeat, our protagonist, a middle manager at a tech firm, finds himself standing at the crossroads of life. He's worked diligently, climbing the corporate ladder from the foundations of software engineering, and is surrounded by the love of his spouse and two children. Yet, with the mounting responsibilities of family, work, and personal aspirations, the weight on his heart, both metaphorically and physically, is palpable.

Though he spends evenings cheering for his favorite football teams, finds solace in occasional video game escapades, and is engrossed in absorbing the wisdom of Joe Rogan and Tim Ferriss, he recognizes a yearning for a more profound sense of health and vitality. And while the culinary delights of heart-healthy foods are a start, he understands that the journey to heart health extends far beyond the plate.

Exercise, as most of us recognize, is pivotal. Not merely for its ability to shed those extra pounds or build muscle definition, but for its profound impact on heart health. For our tech-savvy manager, the idea isn't to become a marathon runner overnight, but to incorporate consistent, moderate exercise into his daily routine. The simple act of choosing stairs over the elevator, enjoying a brisk walk during lunch breaks, or even partaking in morning yoga sessions can significantly enhance cardiovascular health. These aren't herculean tasks but small changes. They're shifts in choice, each pumping more life into the heart, quite literally.

Then there's the domain of mental and emotional well-being. In a world that's more interconnected than ever, the paradox is that feelings of isolation, stress, and burnout are rampant. For a manager overseeing numerous projects and team members, stress is a silent adversary. It's a factor as impactful on heart health as any dietary choice. Engaging in mindfulness practices, meditation, or simply indulging in hobbies like homebrewing or gardening can serve as potent antidotes to the rigors of modern life. They're not just activities but sanctuaries for the heart, allowing it to find its rhythm amid life's cacophonies.

Interestingly, the art of connection, too, plays a pivotal role. Our manager, in the midst of deadlines and family obligations, might find himself secluded from genuine human interactions. Rekindling old friendships, investing quality time with family, or even fostering new relationships can act as balm for the heart. Sharing laughter, reliving memories, or just the simple act of listening and being heard can lower blood pressure, reduce cortisol (stress hormone) levels, and enrich life in ways that are immeasurable.

Speaking of enrichment, the world of continuous learning and personal growth can be an elixir for heart health. It might sound abstract initially, but the sense of accomplishment from mastering a new recipe, understanding the nuances of a challenging concept, or even the joy of reading can stimulate positive emotions, fostering a heart that's not just functioning but thriving.

Sleep, often sidelined, is the unsung hero in the quest for heart health. For someone juggling myriad responsibilities, late nights might be more common than desired. But the heart, like any warrior, needs its rest. Ensuring a consistent sleep schedule, creating a conducive environment for rest, and understanding the body's cues can be transformative. Sleep is when the body heals, recovers, and prepares for the battles of the next day. It's when the heart rejuvenates, ready to take on the world yet again.

In essence, the journey to heart health is multifaceted. It isn't limited to the culinary choices we make, though they are undeniably crucial. It's an orchestration of physical activity, mental well-being, genuine connections, continuous learning, and rejuvenating sleep. For our manager, and indeed for many of us, understanding this holistic approach can be the difference between merely living and truly thriving. As he navigates through the labyrinth of life, with its challenges and triumphs, he's not alone. His heart, bolstered by these practices, beats alongside, robust, resilient, and ready.

From the benefits of physical activity to understanding the importance of stress management

Life in an East Coast city is often likened to the ceaseless beat of a metronome — unwavering, relentless, and charged. For the middle manager at a prominent tech firm, the rhythm is all too familiar. Each morning, as the urban horizon awakens, painted in hues of amber and gold, he sets forth on his daily endeavors. The task of managing teams, overseeing projects, and ensuring the seamless operation of digital wonders is no minor feat. But as the day draws to an end, and he retreats to the solace of his family, a lingering thought often clouds his mind — the silent call for heart health.

The beat of our heart, that rhythmic pulse, is intrinsically tied to the life we lead. From the choices we make at the dining table to the steps we take in the vast urban sprawl, our heart responds, thrives, or merely survives. But understanding heart health is to recognize that it isn't solely about the food we consume. The narrative is far more profound, intertwining the benefits of physical activity with the imperatives of stress management.

Physical activity, in its essence, is the poetry of motion. Each step taken, each muscle flexed, sings praises to the wonders of human anatomy. For our tech-savvy manager, the world of coding and digital marvels may seem miles apart from the realm of physical exertion. But the beauty lies in integration. Incorporating physical activity into daily life doesn't necessitate monumental changes. It begins with choices — simple, yet impactful. Opting for stairs over the elevator, indulging in a morning run, or even adopting the practice of desk exercises can set the foundation. And as the days progress, these choices evolve into habits, each reinforcing the walls of cardiovascular health.

But why is physical activity so paramount? Beyond the obvious benefits of weight management and muscle toning, it serves as the lifeline for the heart. Regular exercise strengthens the heart muscles, improves blood circulation, and significantly reduces the risk of heart diseases. Moreover, it aids in regulating blood pressure, lowering bad cholesterol, and boosting the levels of good cholesterol. It's a symphony of positive repercussions, all stemming from the simple act of moving.

Yet, in the complex tapestry of heart health, physical activity is but one thread. Another, equally significant, is stress management. In the demanding world of tech, where innovations emerge at the speed of thought and deadlines loom like ever-present specters, stress is an unwelcome companion. Its effects, often underestimated, can be detrimental to heart health.

Stress, in its many avatars, triggers the release of adrenaline, causing a spike in blood pressure and heart rate. While the body is designed to handle stress in short bursts, chronic stress can lead to inflammation in the arteries, a precursor to heart disease. It's a silent assailant, often masked by the rigors of daily life.

Understanding stress is one thing, managing it, however, is an art. It begins with self-awareness — recognizing the triggers, understanding personal thresholds, and adopting mechanisms to cope. For our manager, it could be the joy of homebrewing, where the intricate dance of ingredients offers a respite from the digital world. Or perhaps, it's gardening, where amidst the rustle of leaves and the fragrance of blooming flowers, peace finds its way.

Meditation, too, stands as a formidable ally against stress. In the quietude of thought, as breaths deepen and the world fades, the heart finds its rhythm. It's a sanctuary of calm, accessible anytime, anywhere.

Furthermore, the world of media offers avenues to unwind. Perhaps an evening with a Netflix show, a deep dive into a self-help book, or even the intellectual stimulation of podcasts like "The Tim Ferriss Show" can serve as gateways to relaxation. It's about finding balance, understanding that while work is vital, so is the act of unwinding.

In the grand scheme, heart health isn't a destination but a journey. It's a path that meanders through the valleys of physical activity and scales the peaks of stress management. And as our manager navigates this journey, armed with knowledge and fortified by choices, he serves as a beacon for many. For in his quest for heart health, he unravels the tapestry of a life well-lived — where the heart doesn't merely beat but dances with joy.

Chapter 5 "Heart's Best Friends & Foes"

Dive deep into the foods that can be your heart's allies and those that might play foes

In the heart of the bustling East Coast city, where the skyline meets ambition, our tech-savvy middle manager finds himself at a crossroads. While his digital realm is filled with binary codes and software scripts, a different kind of challenge beckons him: understanding the language of his heart through food. Each bite, each morsel, whispers tales of well-being or woe, allies or adversaries. To truly fathom the heart's well-being, it's vital to discern the friends and foes on our plate.

Imagine our manager entering his kitchen after a long day, greeted by the aroma of freshly baked bread, the sizzle of meat on the grill, or the soothing steam of vegetables. The choices he makes here, right in his culinary haven, determine the narrative of his heart's health.

Heart's Allies

Firstly, there's the famed Mediterranean diet, often hailed as the epitome of heart-healthy eating. Think vibrant salads drizzled with olive oil, hearty servings of fatty fish like salmon or mackerel, and the warm embrace of whole grains. Each of these components plays a symphony for the heart.

Fatty fish, for instance, is laden with omega-3 fatty acids, warriors that combat inflammation, reduce blood clotting, and keep heart rhythms stable. As our manager savors the delicate flavors of grilled salmon, perhaps paired with a light quinoa salad, he's not just enjoying a meal; he's fortifying his heart's defenses.

Similarly, nuts, especially almonds and walnuts, emerge as heart's confidantes. Rich in fiber, they also bring along a cocktail of beneficial fats and proteins. A handful as a mid-day snack or sprinkled over a morning oatmeal bowl not only adds texture and flavor but also layers of protection against heart diseases.

Then there's the magic of berries - blueberries, strawberries, raspberries. Beyond their vibrant hues and juicy burst of flavors, they house potent antioxidants. These tiny powerhouses combat oxidative stress, keeping the heart's arteries in prime condition.

Heart's Foes

On the flip side, lurking in the shadows are foods that might seem appealing, even comforting, but play adversaries to heart health. Trans fats, often hidden in the guise of 'hydrogenated oils' in packaged foods, are a heart's nemesis. They raise bad cholesterol, lower the good cholesterol, and amplify the risk of coronary artery disease.

Our manager, while perhaps occasionally tempted by the convenience of fast foods after marathon meetings or late-night coding sessions, must tread with caution. These meals, while satiating, often carry a hefty price tag of saturated fats, sodium, and sugars, all of which, in excess, can strain the heart.

Red meats, especially those processed or laden with fats, pose a similar challenge. They usher in saturated fats that hike up cholesterol levels. So, while the occasional steak or burger can find its way to the dinner table, moderation is the key.

Lastly, the allure of sugary beverages, with their sweet promises, often masks a bitter truth. High sugar intake can lead to weight gain, inflammation, and elevated blood pressure, culminating in unnecessary stress on the heart.

Picture our manager, on a Sunday afternoon, perhaps after watching his favorite football match or diving into a thrilling Netflix series. The decision to whip up a fresh vegetable stir-fry instead of ordering a cheesy pizza, or opting for a refreshing fruit-infused water instead of a soda, defines his allegiance to his heart. Each choice, while seemingly mundane, is a step towards wellness or away from it.

For heart health isn't defined in grand resolutions or colossal changes; it thrives in the minutiae of daily decisions. Every meal, every snack, serves as a dialogue with the heart. And as our tech manager deciphers the language of foods, understanding allies from foes, he doesn't just add days to his life; he adds life to his days.

He becomes an emblem, a testament, to the power of informed choices. For, in the sprawling urban landscape, amidst the challenges of demanding jobs and the joys of family life, lies the opportunity for each of us to be the custodians of our heart's tales, to choose allies and recognize foes. The story of heart health, after all, is penned not in medical journals but in the choices we make, one plate at a time.

Learn the art of grocery shopping for heart wellness and the importance of reading food labels

In the heart of the urban East Coast jungle, the labyrinthine aisles of a grocery store become an arena of choices. For our tech-savvy middle manager, this is not just another chore in the checklist of life. It's an art. The art of grocery shopping for heart wellness. And the compass guiding him through this maze? Food labels.

Imagine him pushing his cart, gliding between aisles, flanked by towers of packaged promises. Each product beckons with the allure of convenience and taste. But buried within these packages, often in fine print, are stories of ingredients and nutrition. Stories that have profound implications for the heart.

The first order of business is to embrace whole foods. Fresh vegetables, fruits, lean meats, whole grains. These are the staples that form the backbone of heart-healthy meals. The colors of bell peppers, the crunch of fresh greens, the sweetness of seasonal fruits – they're not just components of a meal, but heart's trusted allies. Our manager, inspired by his gardening hobby, knows the difference between the fresh dew-kissed produce and the wilted remnants at the back of the shelf. It's not just about freshness, but the vitality these foods infuse into his meals and, by extension, his heart.

However, it's in the middle aisles, where packaged foods reside, that the real challenge emerges. Each box or can, with its vibrant imagery and catchy slogans, poses a riddle. Here, the importance of reading food labels transcends a mere practice – it becomes a critical skill.

Let's consider sodium, for instance. A high intake can be detrimental, escalating blood pressure and heart strain. A cursory glance at a soup can might reveal an enticing flavor profile. But a closer look at its food label might reveal sodium levels that could equate to over half the recommended daily intake. Just one product, one choice, but with profound implications for heart health.

Sugar is another sly culprit. Hidden under aliases like "corn syrup" or "agave nectar", it sneaks into products ranging from cereals to dressings. Our manager, logical and fact-driven as he is, knows the importance of identifying these aliases. By reading and understanding these labels, he's not just choosing a product, he's making an informed decision.

Fat content, especially the types of fat, offers another puzzle. While omega-3s from sources like flaxseed or fish oil are beneficial, trans fats are stark adversaries. Discerning between the two can make the difference between a heart-healthy meal and one that strains the cardiovascular system.

For our manager, each grocery run morphs into a mission. A mission to fortify his pantry with foods that support his heart's well-being. It's not just about filling the cart, but about curating a collection that aligns with his health goals. With every label he reads, every choice he makes, he's scripting a narrative. A narrative of wellness, of informed decisions, of a heart that thrives amidst the urban hustle.

As he checks out, cart laden with colorful produce, lean proteins, and carefully chosen packaged goods, he's not just concluding a shopping trip. He's reaffirming a commitment. A commitment to his heart, to his family, and to a lifestyle that prioritizes well-being even in the heart of the urban jungle. Because in the art of grocery shopping, as in life, it's the choices that define the outcome.

Tips for dining out without compromising heart health

In the vibrant heart of an East Coast city, with its sprawling skyscrapers and bustling streets, the aroma from countless eateries wafts through the air, promising a delectable escape from the daily grind. Our middle manager, after a long week of meetings and code reviews, is drawn to these havens. But dining out, with its myriad choices and hidden ingredients, can often feel like navigating a minefield, especially when heart health is on the line. Yet, with a few strategies up his sleeve, he can savor the city's culinary delights without compromising his heart's well-being.

First and foremost, preparation is key. Before stepping out, he does a quick online recon of the restaurant's menu. With a few taps on his phone, maybe even a quick glance on Reddit's health forums, he can gauge the heart-friendliness of the offerings. Knowing what to expect empowers him to make informed choices, even before he's seated.

Upon arriving, he's not shy about voicing his preferences. In his firm, logical manner, he communicates his dietary needs to the server. It's not about being demanding, but about taking control of his health narrative. Simple requests like "grilled instead of fried" or "dressing on the side" can pivot a meal from being a heart burden to a delightful, guilt-free experience.

Beverages, often the unsung villains, come next. Instead of sugary sodas or overly creamy concoctions, he opts for sparkling water with a splash of lime or a modest glass of red wine, celebrated not just for its rich flavor but also its heart-friendly antioxidants.

When appetizers roll around, he's mindful but not deprived. Instead of the cheese-laden nachos or deep-fried temptations, he leans towards fresh salads, or perhaps a ceviche, savoring the natural flavors and textures that such dishes offer.

Main courses in restaurants are often portioned generously, sometimes excessively. Recognizing this, he listens to his body's cues. Satiety, not a cleaned plate, is his goal. And if the portion is indeed more than what feels right, he's already thinking of the next day's lunch, asking for a takeout box to enjoy the meal again.

But dining out is not just about the food. It's an experience, a sensory journey. Beyond just the plate, he takes in the ambiance, the music, the company. Engaging in lively conversations, perhaps about the latest episode of a show he caught on Netflix or insights from a recent Tim Ferriss podcast, ensures that the pace of the meal is leisurely, allowing for better digestion and appreciation of each bite.

Desserts, while tempting, can often be sugary landmines. He navigates this by either sharing a dessert, curbing the sugar intake, or opting for fruit-based options, which satisfy the sweet tooth while providing beneficial nutrients.

As the evening winds down, and he reflects on the dining experience, it's not one of restriction, but of conscious choices. The joy of savoring the city's culinary offerings remains undiminished, but it's now paired with the satisfaction of knowing that his heart's well-being was never sidelined.

For our middle manager, and indeed for all who seek to balance the pleasures of dining out with health, it's not about saying no, but about saying yes in the right way. And with each mindful choice, he's not just feeding his body, but nourishing his heart, ensuring that the rhythm of life, much like the rhythm of the city he calls home, goes on undeterred.

Conclusion

In the pulsating heart of our urban landscapes, amidst the ebb and flow of modern life, it's no simple task to discern the intricate dance of choices that steer the ship of our health. Chapter 5 has navigated these waters, seeking to demystify the allies and adversaries our hearts encounter daily. In this journey, from the aisles of grocery stores to the tables of city restaurants, our middle manager has become emblematic of us all: trying to harmonize the rhythm of a demanding life with the sacred beat of a healthy heart.

Our protagonist, who began as a software engineer and climbed the ladder of success, is not merely a representation of ambition, but also a testament to evolution. His path reflects an ability to adapt, learn, and grow. In the realm of heart health, he's shown us that the same adaptability, the same thirst for knowledge, can carve out a path that resonates with wellness.

Dive deep we did, into the bounty that nature offers, learning that each morsel we consume can either be a silent guardian or a covert foe to our heart. Understanding this dichotomy is pivotal, not just for the logical, fact-driven mind of our manager, but for anyone wishing to lead a life where the heart doesn't merely exist, but thrives.

The art of grocery shopping evolved from a mundane chore to a strategic endeavor. Each product's label became a story, revealing secrets that could empower decisions. In the matrix of ingredients and nutritional values, there emerged a clear script for heart wellness. One doesn't need to be a gourmet chef or a nutritionist, just an informed individual who knows that every food choice is a brick in the fortress of heart health.

And when the allure of the city's culinary scene beckoned, our middle manager demonstrated that dining out isn't about deprivation, but about discernment. In the space between menu lines, he found the balance of indulgence and insight, proving that the city's gastronomic treasures can be savored without guilt when approached with awareness.

In conclusion, the heart, that tireless drummer, doesn't demand grand gestures. Instead, it thrives on consistent, mindful choices. Our middle manager, in his quest for heart wellness, represents each one of us — battling daily stresses, juggling responsibilities, and yet, aspiring for health. He's shown that with information, intention, and a touch of ingenuity, the path to heart health is not a distant dream but an achievable reality. And in this journey, as in life, it's not the destination but the choices along the way that define our narrative. As the sun sets on the East Coast skyline, one can't help but feel that every heartbeat echoes a story of hope, resilience, and the unwavering pursuit of wellness.

Made in United States
North Haven, CT
24 May 2024

52892091R00067